The United States in the New Global Economy:
A Rallier of Nations

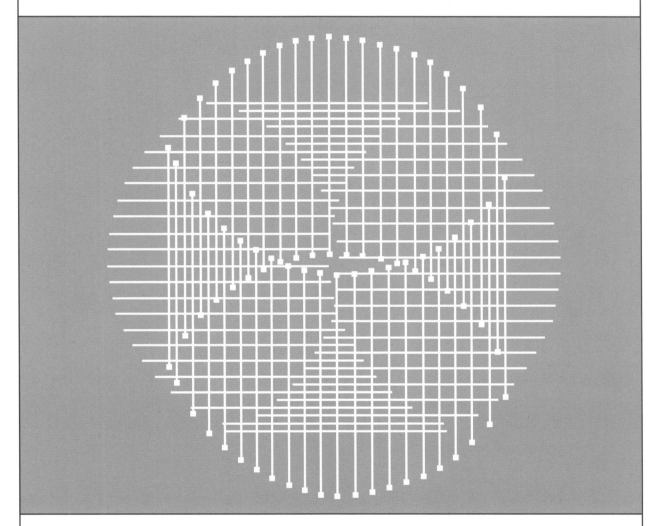

**A Statement by the Research and Policy Committee
of the Committee for Economic Development**

Library of Congress Cataloging-in-Publication Data

The United States in the New Global Economy: A Rallier of Nations /
the Research and Policy Committee of the Committee for Economic
Development.
    p. cm.
    Includes bibliographical references.
     ISBN 0-87186-094-5 : (paperback) : $17.50
    1. United States--Foreign economic relations. 2. International economic
relations. 3. International cooperation. 4. United States--Economic policy--1981-
I. Committee for Economic Development. Research and Policy Committee.
HF1455.U52 1992
337.73--dc20   92-34022
                                                                   CIP

First printing in bound-book form: 1992
Paperback: $17.50
Printed in the United States of America
Design: Rowe & Ballantine

COMMITTEE FOR ECONOMIC DEVELOPMENT
477 Madison Avenue, New York, N.Y. 10022
(212) 688-2063

2000 L Street, N.W., Washington, D.C. 20006
(202) 296-5860

CONTENTS

RESPONSIBILITY FOR CED STATEMENTS ON NATIONAL POLICY

The Committee for Economic Development is an independent research and educational organization of some 250 business leaders and educators. CED is nonprofit, nonpartisan and nonpolitical. Its purpose is to propose policies that bring about steady economic growth at high employment and reasonably stable prices, increased productivity and living standards, greater and more equal opportunity for every citizen, and improved quality of life for all.

All CED policy recommendations must have the approval of trustees on the Research and Policy Committee. This committee is directed under the bylaws which emphasize that "all research is to be thoroughly objective in character, and the approach in each instance is to be from the standpoint of the general welfare and not from that of any special political or economic group." The committee is aided by a Research Advisory Board of leading social scientists and by a small permanent professional staff.

The Research and Policy Committee does not attempt to pass judgment on any pending specific legislative proposals; its purpose is to urge careful consideration of the objectives set forth in this statement and of the best means of accomplishing those objectives.

Each statement is preceded by extensive discussions, meetings, and exchange of memoranda. The research is undertaken by a subcommittee, assisted by advisors chosen for their competence in the field under study.

The full Research and Policy Committee participates in the drafting of recommendations. Likewise, the trustees on the drafting subcommittee vote to approve or disapprove a policy statement, and they share with the Research and Policy Committee the privilege of submitting individual comments for publication.

Except for the members of the Research and Policy Committee and the responsible subcommittee, the recommendations presented herein are not necessarily endorsed by other trustees or by the advisors, contributors, staff members, or others associated with CED.

RESEARCH AND POLICY COMMITTEE

---

*Voted to approve the policy statement but submitted memoranda of comment, reservation, or dissent. (See page 88.)

SUBCOMMITTEE ON A GLOBAL ECONOMIC STRATEGY FOR THE UNITED STATES

*Voted to approve the policy statement but submitted memoranda of comment, reservation, or dissent. (See page 88.)

ADVISORS

PETER B. KENEN
Walker Professor of Economics
    and International Finance
Director, International Finance Section
Princeton University

ROBERT Z. LAWRENCE
Albert L. Williams
Professor of International Trade and
    Investment
John F. Kennedy School of Government
Harvard University

JOSEPH NYE
Director, Center for International Affairs
Harvard University

LAURA D'ANDREA TYSON
Professor of Economics
Research Director
Berkeley Roundtable on the International
    Economy

PROJECT DIRECTOR

LEONARD SILK
Former Economics Columnist
The New York Times

SENIOR PROJECT ADVISOR

ISAIAH FRANK
William L. Clayton Professor of
    International Economics
School of Advanced International Studies
The Johns Hopkins University

PROJECT COUNSELOR

VAN DOORN OOMS
Senior Vice President and Director of
    Research
CED

PROJECT EDITOR

THOMAS L. MONAHAN, III
Director of Editorial Services
CED

PROJECT ASSOCIATE

MICHAEL B. GREENSTONE
Policy Analyst
CED

PROJECT STAFF

CHRIS FLEISCHMAN
EILEEN FORSHEY
TERRA GEIGER
MARIA LUIS
TIM NICHOLS
RAYMUNDO PINEDA
PHIL SCHLAKMAN
JASON SCHOTT

PROJECT FUNDING

The CED project on a Global Economic Strategy for the United States was made possible by generous grants from The Pew Charitable Trusts and The Ford Foundation. Income from the Roy L. Ash Program in American Governance and the Edmund B. Fitzgerald Program in International Studies (generously endowed by Northern Telecom) also supported this project.

CED is also grateful for the generous support of the BankAmerica Corporation, Rockwell International, and the Eastman Kodak Company.

PURPOSE OF THE STATEMENT

As the end of the twentieth century approaches, America confronts a world in the process of profound economic and political change. The superpower rivalry that has guided domestic and international policy has disappeared, seemingly overnight, and with it has gone the singular preeminence of military power as a strategic national asset. The new priority is achieving economic strength to compete effectively in a new global economy and guarantee the prosperity and security of our citizens.

Rather than being acknowledged as remarkable opportunities, these changes seem to have produced a deep pessimism in our society about America's place in this new world. There is widespread concern among the American people that the United States can no longer maintain its position of international leadership and that it lacks the political will to address its pressing domestic needs.

Americans are rightly apprehensive about our nation's economic future and its role in this new world, but CED believes that the United States still has the fundamental strength and vitality to change our national priorities, meet these challenges, and assure future generations of Americans of peace and prosperity. Our success is not guaranteed, however. To achieve these goals we must develop and implement a coherent strategy for adapting national and international community, government, and business institutions to the requirements of this changed world.

CED: VISION FOR A GLOBAL AGE

The Committee for Economic Development's fifty-year history serves as testimony to the power that economic policy, grounded in sound principles and persuasively articulated, can have in fostering economic growth. CED's early work, undertaken in the waning days of World War II, also confronted a world undergoing profound change. Many of the major industrial powers lay in ruins, a military and ideological rivalry with the Soviet Union was beginning to color foreign policy, and nuclear weapons represented a new and daunting threat to our national security.

CED's first trustees found a nation unsure of its prospects in this new world. Depression and mass unemployment were still vivid memories for Americans. To avoid a recurrence of depression, U.S. productivity needed to improve in the first years after the war by 40 percent and private sector employment by an additional 20 percent over 1940 levels. At the same time, the world trading system no longer existed, and most of the Western economies were devastated. The nation was at a crossroad. The correct policy might lead the country to years of unheralded prosperity and peace. The wrong action might return the nation to the awful days of the Great Depression.

Whether designing policies for the reconstruction of Europe, the world trading system, or conversion of the domestic economy, CED's trustees tested their recommendations by some very fundamental and far-reaching standards. On international policy, the trustees asked whether their recommendations lent themselves to:

- The preservation of peace and the reduction of international discord and ill-will
- The safeguarding and extension of free cultural, political, and economic institutions
- The achievement of progressively higher levels of material well-being for people worldwide

The trustees judged the benefits of domestic policy by the following criteria, which sound all too familiar today:

- What are our prospects for steady employment and income?

- What are the risks that inflation will reduce the power of our income and savings?

- Will we and our children experience during our lifetime a continuing improvement of our standard of living as much as our parents and grandparents did?

With these goals in mind, CED's founders carefully considered the key elements of an integrated strategy, issuing simultaneous policy statements on postwar employment and reform of the world trading system and other reports that addressed the important national and international economy policy issues of the day.

These statements made a range of recommendations, and detailed the institutional arrangements needed to carry them out. The 1945 policy statements *International Trade, Foreign Investment and Domestic Employment* and *The Bretton Woods Proposals* played a key role in the creation of the International Bank for Reconstruction and Development (later the World Bank) and the International Monetary Fund. *Toward More Production, More Jobs and More Freedom* (1946) served as the basis for CED's active involvement in the creation of the Employment Act of 1946 and the establishment of the President's Council of Economic Advisers and the Joint Economic Committee of Congress.

Over the years, CED's policy statements have continued to confront the pressing economic issues of our time. In the past decade, CED has uniquely positioned itself to consider how the United States needs to respond to today's challenges. CED's recommendations, which are guided by the same principles that guided its early work, constitute a strategy designed to maintain U.S. competitive strength.

We have advocated a macroeconomic policy designed to result in lower federal budget deficits, increased saving and capital investment, greater productivity, and stable long-term noninflationary growth; a regulatory policy that does not limit the ability of

U.S. business to compete internationally; a strategy to facilitate industrial and regional labor market adjustment; a life-cycle approach to boosting the quality of the nation's human resources; and policy for combating unfair trading practices without endangering the world trading system.

CED has continued its support for an open world economy while recommending fair treatment for U.S. industry in foreign markets. *Breaking New Ground in U.S. Trade Policy* (1991) developed a stair-step trade strategy through which U.S. policy makers could combat unfair trade without jeopardizing multilateral trade agreements. CED has conducted discussions with its counterpart organizations in Europe, Australia, and Japan to identify and address possible threats to the system of international trade. A recent series of discussions with Keizai Doyukai (the Japan Association of Corporate Executives) produced the joint statement *Strengthening U.S.-Japan Economic Relations: An Action Program for the Public and Private Sectors* (1989). CED has also spelled out much-needed principles for investment in less developed countries, whose integration into the global economy will be a top priority in the coming years.

CED has often focused on those elements of the domestic economy that allow the United States to maintain a high standard of living and consistent economic growth. Recent statements on education and child development, *Investing in Our Children, Children in Need,* and *The Unfinished Agenda,* have put CED at the forefront of a national movement to renew America's commitment to its children. To boost the quality of America's work force, CED's work on demographics and jobs has articulated a comprehensive human-investment strategy: the life-cycle approach to the U.S. work force outlined in *An America that Works* (1990). CED's ground-breaking statement *Work and Change* (1987) outlined a plan for easing the transition of workers dislocated by a changing labor market.

CED has long sought to build national support for sound federal fiscal policy, maintaining that the federal budget should be in balance or have a small surplus in times of high employment. Recent CED statements such as *Politics, Tax Cuts, and the Peace Dividend* (1991) and *The Economy and National Defense* (1991) have stressed that the growing federal budget deficits of the past decade have damaged prospects for economic growth and weakened U.S. competitiveness.

A NEW ROLE FOR AMERICA

The trustees of CED prepared this policy statement because they believe that designing sound policy for a changed world is a fitting way to commemorate CED's fiftieth anniversary. *The United States in the New Global Economy: A Rallier of Nations* was developed by a CED subcommittee composed of leading business executives and scholars. The statement defines a new role for America as a "rallier of nations," in which the United States embraces responsibility for stimulating cooperative international action and helps create the new rules and institutional arrangements needed to generate and distribute wealth in an interdependent world.

As a rallier of nations, the United States needs to promote international coordination of domestic policies, particularly in such critical areas as fiscal and monetary measures, trade and investment promotion, energy development and conservation, environmental protection, and collective security. These commitments will lead to new post cold war rules and institutional arrangements to govern international relations and build trust between countries.

The United States must also move intelligently and quickly to adapt its own economic priorities to reflect the demands of a changed world. U.S. business needs to reshape its own practices, to become more flexible and innovative. Government, business, labor, and academia must form a new domestic partnership, a cooperative effort aimed at keeping America competitive into the next century.

Finally, this new role has created a different reality for policy makers in government and business. Gone are the walls separating domestic from foreign affairs. The new reality of global interdependence requires a new way of thinking about national agendas, one in which successful actions are judged by how they advance the ability of citizens in our country, other developed countries, and developing countries to produce and prosper in a global economy.

Now that communism has collapsed and the cold war is at an end, the spotlight is turned on market systems and democracy. America must articulate a sense of direction and purpose that inspires the American people and the citizens of other nations to move boldly into the twenty-first century.

ACKNOWLEDGMENTS

I would like to express CED's gratitude to our ten international counterpart organizations (listed at the back of the report). We had the opportunity to share the report with them at various stages in its development, and the comments and suggestions improved the report immeasurably.

I would like to express the deep appreciation of the Research and Policy Committee to A. W. Clausen, Chairman of the Executive Committee at BankAmerica and Chairman of the CED Subcommittee on a Global Economic Strategy for the United States, for his leadership and enthusiasm in directing the development of this statement. The breadth and complexity of the topic posed a difficult challenge. The Chairman and the Subcommittee on a Global Economic Strategy for the United States (listed on page vi) therefore deserve a special commendation for bringing this project to a successful conclusion in a very brief time.

I would also like to acknowledge the special efforts of the project director Leonard Silk, former economics columnist of *The New York Times*, for crafting such an eloquent assessment of the changes shaping the world and a prescription for a U.S. response. A note of thanks is also due Isaiah Frank of Johns Hopkins, CED's Advisor on International Economic Policy, and Sandra Kessler Hamburg, CED's Vice President and Director Of

Education Studies, for their roles in shaping the statement. Project editor Tom Monahan and project associate Michael Greenstone, both of the CED staff, also merit special mention for their contributions to this report.

And, most important, thanks are due to my predecessor as Chairman of CED's Research and Policy Committee, Dean P. Phypers. The quality and breadth of work done during Dean's tenure speak for themselves, but it was truly a remarkable achievement to have brought a project as comprehensive as this to such a successful conclusion.

Josh S. Weston
Chairman
CED Research and Policy Committee

CHAPTER 1

INTRODUCTION AND STATEMENT OF PRINCIPLES

Since the end of the cold war and the onset of recession, the dialogue on future American global involvement has increasingly been tinged with isolationist sentiments. Haunted by seemingly intractable domestic problems and a seemingly diminished competitive position internationally, numerous U.S. public officials and opinion leaders have urged the United States to reconsider its commitment of resources to international issues and its advocacy of open markets at home and abroad. In the heat of this year's election politics, we have seen this theme repeated again and again.

This budding isolationism ignores the substantial and continuing benefits of U.S. international leadership. People worldwide have been the beneficiaries of U.S. international leadership, but none more so than the citizens of the United States, who have enjoyed decades of unprecedented growth and security. Those who argue that we can retreat from our position of world leadership without suffering serious consequences fail to recognize the increasingly interdependent nature of the world economy or the U.S. ability to compete effectively in it.

Our domestic well-being has become inseparably connected to that of the world around us. Between exports of products and services and direct foreign investment in the United States, millions of American jobs are tied to the global economy. Our ability to compete effectively in this world market — as individuals, as businesses, and as a nation — is essential to our prosperity and quality of life. Achieving our goals, both domestic and international, will require recognizing that the prosperity of Americans is inseparably connected to the new global economy.

Participation in the global economy has helped to foster remarkable American economic growth. Greater economic interdependence among the major industrial nations has helped them to avoid catastrophic war for nearly fifty years. Most important, it was our economic strength that allowed us to triumph in the cold war, and eliminated the Soviet Union as a major threat to security. Because the United States has a strong interest in the further integration of the international economy and how it is achieved, we need to maintain our position of international leadership. And because the world has undergone dramatic change, the United States must redefine its leadership role accordingly.

LEADERSHIP AND CHANGE

The United States today is not the single dominant power of the free world that it was at the end of World War II. The economic strength of Japan and the other nations of the Pacific Rim and the burgeoning economic power of a more integrated Europe make it unlikely that this nation will be in that position again.

Now the United States must seek a new leadership role, not as the only dominant power, but as a rallier of nations in a world in which power and wealth are more widely diffused. Leadership and a coherent strategy will remain crucial to identifying and furthering the common interests of all countries. Size and military power will continue as important sources of America's international influence. But, as the turbulent events of the recent past have demonstrated, other abilities and attributes will become more critical in helping this nation to provide international leadership.

In the next century, the United States must become a catalyst of change in national attitudes and behavior, in scientific and technological advancement, and in enabling international institutions to safeguard the peace and to further economic development. That is the role we should seek as a rallier of nations. Other nations and regions have developed into rival economic powers, and we need to work closely with them. But no other nation can muster the combination of military, economic, and political influence needed for world leadership. The contrasting responses of the West to the problems in the Persian Gulf and in former Yugoslavia dramatically illustrate the need for a decisive nation capable of spearheading international action.

Our task is to safeguard what we have gained at such enormous cost in this century and to help move the world forward into the new century. We do not have the option of isolating ourselves from the rest of the world. The emergence of powerful transnational business and financial institutions, the speed of electronic communications, and the diffusion of new scientific and technological knowledge now ensure that our interests cannot be separated from those of other nations.

However, America's effective performance as a leader is not a foregone conclusion. Our economy and society are plagued with a number of serious problems, ranging from social welfare to education to huge budget deficits to inadequate investment in our own future, that threaten to erode our competitiveness and stability. The recent disturbances in Los Angeles make all too clear the problems that we must confront as a nation. These conditions have fueled anxieties that a U.S. decline from leadership is inevitable. We reject such pessimism and fatalism; these qualities have never been part of the American character. If we can come to terms with the problems we face at home, our open, pluralistic, multiethnic, free-market society will give us distinct advantages as a leader. As the world's foremost example of a multiethnic democracy, the United States can serve as a compelling model for nations coming to grips with ethnic strife.

The international business community has become a crucial contributor to global change. By operating on market principles, business can outpace government and international institutions in responding to emerging trends. So, too, in the marketplace of ideas, business must probe and evaluate the new issues that nations will face. Through its worldwide role, business can bring fresh perspectives and vital resources to the task of building a global economy.

STATEMENT OF KEY PRINCIPLES

From our business experience and our year-long study of emerging trends, we conclude that six key principles should guide U.S. policy in the global age. Taken together, these principles provide a new collective agenda for the community of nations and a domestic foundation for sustained prosperity and leadership:

Toward a safer and more prosperous world:

- **Although the United States still has an important international role to play as guarantor of peace and stability, its military forces should be reduced to reflect diminishing threats to international security. At the same time, the United States should begin to develop collective security agreements with other nations that will ensure a more equitable distribution of military responsibilities and costs. This pattern of cooperative effort should also be extended to nonmilitary threats to the community of nations.**

- **The United States should continue to be a champion of free and open commerce between sovereign nations. Open markets and a global flow of capital and services are the surest way to promote economic growth and foster peace.**

- **The end of the cold war offers the industrial nations a unique opportunity to promote sustainable economic growth in the developing world. The most developing nations will experience remarkable population growth in the years ahead, and their economic viability should be of substantial commercial and humanitarian concern to the United States.**

Toward a stronger American economy and society:

- **Reduction of huge U.S. federal budget deficits should be the highest domestic economic priority. Deficits erode U.S.**

competitiveness and prospects for future economic growth by absorbing national savings that could be used for productive investment and by raising the cost of capital. The government should shift federal policy away from encouraging consumption and toward favoring productive saving and investment.

- **While maintaining a strong and mobile military force, the United States should shift its policy emphasis from military strength to economic strength, the vital component of world leadership in the decades ahead.**

- **In a world economy shaped by rapid global dissemination of major technological advances, where businesses are free to locate centers of production or service anywhere, the quality of a nation's human capital will become the single most important determinant of its prosperity. With this in mind, the United States should pursue a comprehensive human-investment strategy that begins before every birth and continues throughout our working lives.**

Following these mutually reinforcing principles will require new patterns of cooperation among both sovereign nations and segments of American society. We recognize that these six principles, and the more detailed recommendations that follow, do not address every single challenge that the United States and its partners abroad will confront in the coming years. Instead, as a panel of business leaders, we sought to identify the most pressing *economic* issues facing the community of nations, and to outline the U.S. role in addressing them. To meet the challenges of the post cold war world and the integrated global economy, the United States must be ready to carve out a new role for itself in the community of nations. In order to lay the economic foundations for this role, American business, government, labor, and the American people must adapt their own perspectives and begin to collaborate on creating a growing, productive and competitive America.

CHAPTER 2

THE UNITED STATES AND GLOBAL CHANGE

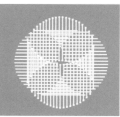

Our global experiences in the past three years have ranged from the collapse of communism and the drive toward democracy and economic freedom to the shock of war. What lessons have we learned that will help us realize our hopes for a peaceful and prosperous world in the years ahead? The sudden changes that have shaken societies and economies all over the world have both disturbed and elated us. Now, in the midst of these revolutionary developments, we seem poised on the threshold of a new world as nations remake themselves, old alliances fall apart, and new coalitions are forged.

Although these changes are startling, equally meaningful developments are subtly and profoundly reshaping our world. International commerce continues to erode the significance of national boundaries. A global flow of people, capital, services, and products is altering relationships between metropolitan areas, nations, and regions. As the Soviet Union has disintegrated and imperial communism has receded as a threat to world security, military power is being replaced by economic power as a measure of strength and influence among nations. But even as economic interests and technological advances seem to be pulling the nations of the world closer together, the collapse of the Soviet Union and the breakdown of the postwar bipolar system has unleashed disintegrative forces. In a world less threatened by superpower rivalry, national, regional, and ethnic priorities have changed substantially in a short period of time.

It is precisely because of this increased interdependence that the world cannot allow the disintegrative forces to prevail. A new pattern of international relations that is based on cooperative agreement and burden sharing will help the world to maintain past gains and continue to prosper in the future.

With all these astonishing changes, one thing has not changed at all: The United States still possesses qualities — unique in the community of nations — that allow it to influence events worldwide through diplomacy, economic pressure, and leadership in international institutions. American leadership is especially qualified to help develop collective agendas for international action that can subsume divergent national interests.

For America to assume this role in the future, however, it will have to effectively address a number of problems at home. The list of domestic issues that require strong leadership includes: eliminating the federal budget deficit, ensuring that all U.S. citizens receive a quality education and are prepared to successfully enter the work force, ensuring that opportunities for success are available to all Americans, and creating an environment in which productive enterprise and innovation will flourish.

U.S. INTERESTS IN AN INTEGRATED GLOBAL ECONOMY

From an economic standpoint, the world is becoming borderless. By necessity, the leading corporations take a global perspective; they produce goods and services, source their supplies and talent, market their products; conduct research and development, and locate their facilities wherever in the world it is most profitable. World financial markets now operate twenty-four hours a day. Capital flows between countries and continents on a massive basis, and instantaneous communications have relentlessly accelerated the conduct of international commerce.

The United States still has the most powerful and diverse economy in the world, but its well-being is increasingly linked to that of other nations by these worldwide flows of products, services, capital, and ideas. Although it is largely the product of technological progress and a recognition of the benefits it offers to participants, much of this integration of the global economy has been aided by deliberate U.S. government policy. Since World War II, the United States has fostered the development of economic links between nations in the belief that deeper integration of the world economy would be of the greatest benefit both to U.S. citizens and to our trading partners. U.S. policy makers have also believed that economic interdependence would limit future armed conflict.

At the same time, U.S. businesses played a vital role in creating the world economy. Major U.S. corporations developed world markets for their products, using a combination of exports and direct foreign investment. In the process, they transformed themselves into multinational enterprises with interests and responsibilities the world over.

Just as the market economies have demonstrated their superiority over centrally planned economies, so has the liberalization of international trade and investment proven its advantages over closed systems in enhancing the efficiency of the world economy. Since the end of World War II, the United States has been a vigorous leader in pushing for open markets. It has taken this position not only to promote its own interests but also to work for the benefits of the world as a whole, especially the developing world. During this period, trade, investment, and output have grown at historically unprecedented rates, as nations and industries benefited from economies of scale, increased competition, and a more rational deployment of resources.

These deepening bonds among the economies of individual nations have had several consequences.

1. **Worldwide Economic Growth and General Improvement in Living Standards**. In economic terms, open markets for goods, services, and capital are the best means of achieving broad-based improvements in economic welfare. World markets promote specialization by encouraging nations and businesses to make the goods and services that they produce best and to buy what others produce best. By forcing producers to compete against the best in the world, open markets also encourage innovation and efficiency. A worldwide flow of capital helps ensure that resources are put to their most productive uses.

Although the increasing globalization of commerce has produced remarkable gains for the world as a whole, these gains have not been evenly distributed. Nations that actively participated in the more open world market have fared far better than those nations, most notably those South Asian and sub-Saharan African nations that have seen their economies stagnate and their poverty worsen.

2. **Increased Political Stability**. The United States was the major international advocate of a liberalized world trading system after World War II because it correctly affirmed that increased economic interdependence would help stave off catastrophic global conflict. Although regional conflicts have at times threatened to escalate into superpower confrontations, the world has been spared conflagrations on the scale of the two world wars. Experience has shown that market democracies, with economies tied to the world around them, tend not to go to war with one another.

As the European Community (EC) completes its transformation into a single internal market, it is worth remembering that the Community's primary objective in creating an integrated economic structure was political stability. The EC has already accomplished this objective and stands ready to reap significant economic benefits if it can achieve internal integration without shutting out the rest of the world. But the Community's recent experiences also demonstrate how difficult it can be to convince individual nations to surrender some control over their own economies.

3. **Economic Growth on the Part of Our Competitors and Trading Partners**. Increased international business activity has served as a conduit to other sections of the world for American technology and management techniques, two foundations of U.S. postwar economic dominance. Access to the vast and lucrative U.S. market has also enabled other nations, especially Japan and Germany, to attain rapid growth. As can be seen from Figure 1, since 1960, real GDP per worker doubled

in Germany and quadrupled in Japan, enabling these nations to compete more broadly with the United States. Having robust trading partners and competitors is not unhealthy; part of their success can even be traced to the deliberate American policy of fostering strong industrial democracies to create a bulwark against imperial communism. These same nations can now play an important role in crafting cooperative efforts to address global problems.

4. **A Remarkably High Standard of Living and Decades of Economic Growth for the United States**. Access to foreign markets and the availability of foreign products, ideas, and capital have substantially raised the quality of life in the United States over the past fifty years. American participation in the global economy has enabled three generations of Americans to enjoy rapidly rising standards of living in a more secure world. However, the benefits of integration have not been distrib-

uted evenly. In the past decade, lower-skilled American workers have seen real wages decline under pressure from foreign competitors.[1]

Our domestic economy and our national well-being are now inseparably connected to this global economy. One fifth of our corporations' profits come from their overseas activities. One in six manufacturing jobs relies on exports, and 25 percent of our agricultural output is sold overseas.[2] Whether exported or not, 70 percent of U.S. manufacturing output now faces direct foreign competition.

The United States is both the world's largest importer and exporter. Figure 2 reveals that U.S. imports and exports as a percentage of GDP have more than doubled since 1960. In addition, foreign investment in the U.S. has grown more than sevenfold since 1976, increasing from $281 billion to more than $2 trillion. U.S. investment abroad has grown nearly 400 percent since 1970 (See Figure 3).

Stronger ties to the international marketplace have benefited Americans in a variety of other ways. Strong foreign enterprises have forced U.S companies to excel and have supplied U.S. enterprises with competitive component parts. American consumers have enjoyed a wider choice of products and better quality. Interaction with other cultures even provides Americans with a range of opportunities that enrich our economy and improve our quality of life.

DISINTEGRATIVE THREATS

This economic integration has taken place at a much faster rate than political adaptation to the increasing interdependence of modern industrial nations. Even as forces bind national economies closer together, threats to the continuing integration of the world economy — and hence to the well-being of individual nations — loom on the horizon. For all the benefits that interdependence has produced, it has also produced significant fear of change. Despite the benefits, some nations have responded with nationalistic cries for retreat from the rigors of interdependence via increased protection.

The most daunting of these would be the breakdown of the open world trading system,

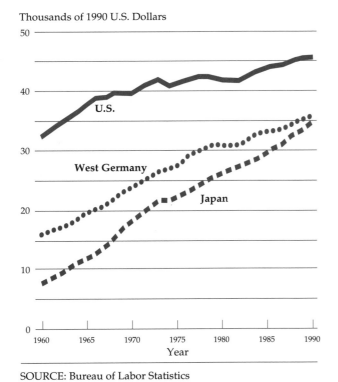

Figure 1

Real GDP Per Worker, Selected Nations

Thousands of 1990 U.S. Dollars

U.S.

West Germany

Japan

SOURCE: Bureau of Labor Statistics

Figure 2

U.S. Exports and Imports

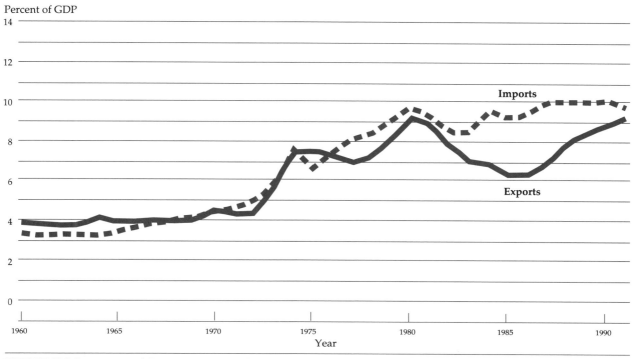

Percent of GDP

SOURCE: U.S. Department of Commerce, Bureau of Economic Analysis

which the United States led the way in creating after World War II. That system, embodied in the principles of the General Agreement on Tariffs and Trade (GATT), has been endangered by the rise of protectionist pressures in many countries, pressures intensified by the recession in the United States and the slowdown of the world economy. In fact, twenty of the twenty four countries that make up the Organization for Economic Cooperation and Development (OECD) have increased trade barriers in the past decade. If protectionist pressures should cause a breakdown in world trade, we could face a global depression, as happened during the early 1930s. Such a collapse would have especially dire consequences for the United States.

Some see a threat to continued interdependence from the increasing internal preoccupations around the globe. For instance, although the merger of West and East Germany is a great gain for democracy, it also means that Europe will be intensely concerned with its own integration as well as its relations with its stable neighbors in the European Community and its less stable neighbors to the East. Concurrently, there have been signals that the United States sees the end of the cold war as a chance to turn inward and concentrate on its domestic agenda. Japan's increasing focus on investment in Asia suggests that if it is spurned by Europe and the United States, it will retreat from its global orientation.

Many contend that the emergence of regional trade groups in Europe, North America, and the Far East are a manifestation of this increasing introspection. However, regional groupings aimed at economic and political integration do not necessarily threaten the world trading system, provided that they do not split the world into hostile and protectionist trade blocs. If regional groups remain open to the outside world, they can in fact reduce trade barriers and spur both regional and world economic growth.[3] Unfortunately, the nature of these arrangements has not yet been completely defined. The protectionist rumblings that are affecting political debate both in the United States and abroad could do real harm to both the global system and national economies.

In the United States, this revival of protectionist sentiment springs from the concern of American workers who will face increased global competition. They fear that in a world where products and capital can flow more freely, U.S. workers will be replaced by cheaper foreign labor. During the 1980's, lower skill U.S. workers did in fact see a decline in income due to more intense foreign competition.[4] Businesses, however, take a number of factors into account when deciding where to base their production of goods and services: proximity to key markets, infrastructure, and local taxes all play important roles. But the most important determinant is the productivity of an area's labor measured against its cost. Hence, countries with more expensive labor, such as Germany and Japan, are still among our fiercest competitors because of the high productivity of their work forces. Conversely, some developing nations with remarkably low wage rates have consistently failed to attract capital investment because their productivity is low.

United States policy makers are correct to be apprehensive about the prospects of current and future generations of Americans, but retreating from world markets will certainly not ensure prosperity. Instead of isolating our economy, the United States should attempt to become an attractive location for productive investment from either domestic or foreign investors. A number of ways that U.S. policy makers can help achieve this are outlined in Chapter 4.

THE UNITED STATES AND WORLD SECURITY

The collapse of the Soviet Union has left the United States as the world's most powerful nation in military terms. But even as the emergence of a one-power world has introduced a new order into security relations, some disintegrative threats to security have appeared. The proliferation of weapons, both nuclear and

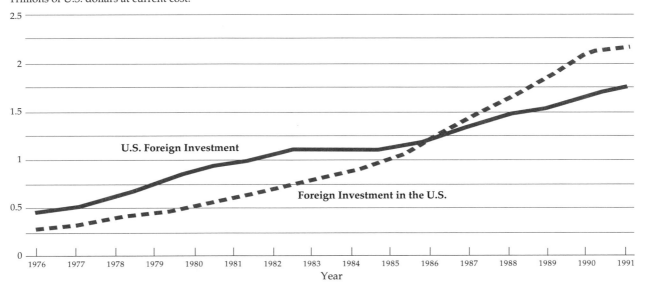

Figure 3

U.S. Foreign Investment Position
1976-91

Trillions of U.S. dollars at current cost.

SOURCE: 1976, Survey of Current Business. June, 1991; 1977-91, Survey of Current Business, June, 1992.

conventional, has given otherwise weak states the power to threaten global peace. The war in the Persian Gulf was a dramatic example of the havoc that well-armed smaller countries can wreak. Iraq's aggression against its neighbors endangered not only those countries, but a world economy still dependent on Middle Eastern oil. That threat could recur, whether driven by dictatorial ambitions, the anti-Western hostility of religious fundamentalism, or other nationalist and ideological forces.

A second threat to world political and economic stability was unleashed by the disintegration of the Soviet Union. Although the end of the cold war has increased the possibility of lasting peace and world economic growth, it has also unleashed nationalist and ethnic conflicts that had been repressed by Soviet power. If the breakup of the Soviet empire leads to an economic catastrophe, spreading unemployment, collapsing living standards, famine, and disease, it could bring back dictatorships, aggravate nationalist and ethnic conflicts, and endanger the West, as well. As then Secretary of State James Baker said in his Princeton University address: "We are not the leaders of this revolution, but neither are we mere bystanders; we are models for its leaders, we are partners in its progress, and we can be beneficiaries of its success for decades to come. Yet the time for action is short. History is giving no one breathing space."[5]

The collapse of the USSR has removed the threat of Soviet aggression but released powerful nationalist antagonisms not only in the former Soviet republics and Eastern Europe, but also in other parts of the globe. The cold war had provided a surcease from aggressive nationalism by causing countries to seek protection under the Soviet or American umbrella. Reemergence of nationalist impulses in the decomposed Soviet empire is not surprising. Hitler and Stalin dealt with the Eastern European boundaries and sovereignties as though they were trading chits. After 1945, nations were smothered by Soviet power. Now, after half a century of repression, it is small wonder that the age-old issue of national identity has arisen with such fury. Economic stability and effective diplomacy can help ameliorate these tensions.

Despite its strained finances, the United States must continue to play an active role in the new Europe that is emerging. The situation that faces the United States in Europe today is without precedent. But if the new Europe is to solidify and make a lasting contribution to world security, it must find a way of living and working with the successor states of the Soviet empire, of which Russia will be the most powerful. An isolated and beleaguered Russia has never been a well-behaved member of the international community. There is broad recognition in Europe and the United States that if the Russians feel unduly vulnerable the security of the West might be in jeopardy. It is far too soon to conclude that we shall have no further trouble from that sector, that the job is done and the United States can "go home." A continued American military presence, albeit at a lower level, will help to stabilize this area.

Most important, the threat of nuclear terror is not dead. In the Pacific, the Japanese live next to two nuclear powers, China and Russia. Another near-neighbor, North Korea, may soon achieve nuclear capability. Particularly given Japan's understandable aversion to military action, a continued American security guarantee should serve as a significant deterrent to hostilities in the Pacific. The proliferation of nuclear weapons to countries with histories of aggression also presents a potential problem. In the face of the ongoing dangers from the former Soviet Union's 25,000 nuclear warheads, only the United States can lead in the arms control negotiations and arms reductions that will be needed to turn fragile global ties into genuine stability.

The collapse of the Soviet Union and its military threat to the West, superimposed on the deepening integration of the global economy, necessitates a rethinking of U. S. strategy to deal with the problems and opportunities of a radically changed world. Even after making relatively optimistic assumptions about the reduced Soviet threat and successful negotiation of future arms control and reduction agreements, America will continue to have to direct significant resources toward maintaining an adequate defense of our national interests. **Although America will still be the** largest military force in the post cold war world, it cannot become the global policeman. Rather, as a rallier of nations, the United States should seek to insure that the international community increase its reliance on the United Nations and other supranational organizations, even as we exert our influence to make them function more effectively.

The war in the Persian Gulf, though an immediate military success, might not become the precise model for America's future role in relation to other countries. Arrangements to deal with the crisis were necessarily ad hoc, but they represented the first steps toward more powerful collaborative arrangements. To facilitate future cooperation, the international community should approve the establishment of collective security structures capable of responding quickly to future threats and ensuring a fair distribution of the burdens of action.*

SECURING VICTORY IN THE COLD WAR

One of the first acts of any collective arrangement must be to abet the peaceful transition of the former Soviet republics to democratic market economies. **As we did after World War II (unlike after World War I) in helping both our friends and our defeated enemies, the United States should strive to aid the reconstruction of Eastern Europe and the republics of the Commonwealth of Independent States (CIS).** Rescuing the former Communist countries from economic ruin is a security issue of great importance. Achieving political and economic stability, eliminating nuclear weapons, and bringing the new Eastern states into the free world could provide the basis for a lasting peace.

For a variety of reasons, the decision to aid the former Soviet Union is separate from our reconsideration of aid to the developing world (see page 45). The first and perhaps most compelling reason for a different course of action is that we may have only a narrow window of opportunity for supporting democratic reform in Russia and the other nations of the Commonwealth of Independent States.

Second, the development of peaceful and prosperous economies in Russia and the other former Soviet states has direct national security implications for the United States. Four of these states have substantial nuclear capabilities, making them a nuclear threat to our own safety, in addition to being a conventional threat to our allies in Europe.

Third, Russia and the other former Soviet republics face some unique challenges (and have some unique advantages) that will require Western nations to use a different approach in aiding their development. In planning our strategy for aid, we need to remember that the former Soviet republics are states at widely varying levels of development. But unlike the developing world, some of these nations are industrialized economies. Although most of their physical capital will need to be modernized and redirected toward civilian use and their managers will need to respond to the demands of the marketplace rather than centralized state control, the challenge these states face is as much one of transition as of outright development. These states also possess a formidable number of skilled scientists whose talents have largely been applied to military technology but could be a substantial advantage in a technology-driven global economy. In addition, because the state system often apportioned technology and capital unevenly among the various republics, leaders in these new states need to create not only market economies but also independent economies.

THE GOALS OF AID

The United States, Japan, and the other industrialized countries must put major emphasis on internal economic, legal, and institutional reforms by the republics; this will be essential to ensure that Western aid is not wasted or even counterproductive. Yet, aid from the West will be a crucial element in facilitating internal reforms, as it was in Europe after World War II. Technical missions of the United States, the European Community (EC), the United Nations, the World Bank, and the International Monetary Fund (IMF) can do much to guide their macroeconomic and microeconomic policies for reconstruction, currency reform, and more rational economic

---

*See memoranda by RODERICK M. HILLS, (page 88).

relations with each other and the rest of the world. Coordinated aid programs will have the advantage of avoiding clashes among the industrialized countries for a dominant position in the East.

Although dispensing aid quickly is a high priority, the West needs to be vigilant in assuring that its money is well spent. Accordingly, we suggest the following guidelines for continuing aid:

Reducing the security threat, both conventional and nuclear, to the community of nations, and ensuring that the former Soviet republics do not harm the global environment. International monetary and technical assistance should be directed toward helping Russia to dismantle weapons of mass destruction, reduce its stockpile of nuclear weapons and promote nuclear safety in the Soviet power industry. Efforts should also be made to put Russian scientists to productive work before their knowledge can be exploited by nations pursuing nuclear technology.

Fostering internal and external political stability and sound economic development in the region. To ensure that it does not perpetuate need, aid should encourage reform of economic and political systems. In the near term, humanitarian aid should ease the hardship of transition to a market economy to sustain public support for reform. In the longer term, aid should help lay the foundation for self-sufficient free-market economies and sound strategies for lasting economic growth. At the same time, since much of the capital needed to finance the transition will have to come from private investors, the republics should adopt policies that encourage and facilitate private investment. Linking the former Soviet republics to the international economy as quickly as their economies will allow will benefit all nations.

STRATEGIES FOR ASSISTANCE

We applaud the leadership of the IMF in assembling a pool of capital to aid the former Soviet republics and urge the U.S. government, both the Administration and Congress, to make good on U.S. commitments to the multilateral aid efforts. Although we should rely primarily on the IMF, the World Bank, and the European Bank for Reconstruction and Development (EBRD) to direct Western assistance to where it can do the most good, the United States must be ready to shoulder its share of the financial burden. Moreover, the reconstruction of the former Soviet states should not divert resources from problems in the less developed nations. The integration of the CIS nations into the global economy is an additional challenge, and it will require additional expenditures.

Strengthening the lending capacity of the IMF. The IMF has recognized that as the CIS and Eastern European nations attempt to make the transition to becoming market economies, demands on IMF resources will increase. In order to meet this rise in demand, the IMF has requested a 50% increase in its lending reserves from $120 billion to $180 billion. The IMF's Board of Governors (with the support of the United States) approved this increase and agreed to appropriate it by December 31, 1991. Although originally slow to honor the U.S. commitment, Congress has recently appropriated the necessary funding.

Even without the increase in loan reserves, the IMF had already assembled a pool of Western capital to achieve the first priority — stabilizing the ruble. But new capital is still desperately needed for two other objectives:

• *Enabling the CIS nations to import needed food, supplies, and components*. This aid, much of which is in the form of import credits, would also directly benefit Western exporters, who would gain early access to the CIS market.

• *Meeting foreign debt payments*. If the transformation into a prosperous market economy succeeds, this money could be repaid. In the interim, however, foreign governments could also help development by working to lighten the burden of foreign debt.

Although it is critically important for the United States to act swiftly and decisively to help administer needed capital, American business and government can take other important steps to ensure a stable transition to freedom for the former Soviet states.

Humanitarian Aid. The transition into free-market economies will inflict severe pain on the former Soviet people in the short run. The United States and the Western nations can relieve some of this pain and shore up popular support for reform, by distributing food and medicine to the former Soviet peoples. To ensure that such aid addresses real need, the West should be ready to supply logistical help in assuring its proper distribution.

Technical Assistance (Both in Management and in Governance). Much attention has been focused on the amount of direct aid being steered towards the countries of the former Soviet Union. Although capital is greatly needed, providing proper guidance for economic reform is equally important. Former Soviet industries face tremendous difficulties in their transition to freestanding organizations because of the fundamental differences between centrally planned economies and market competition. Facing a competitive market requires new thinking on the part of managers and government officials in these nations.

Although investments in the CIS economies will support local enterprises and help to create new ones, they will soon vanish if they fail to compete effectively. One possible form for this type of assistance is a Peace Corps like organization of Western managers. American business, which has long "loaned" managers to nonprofit domestic initiatives, may have incentives for paying executives' salaries while they participate in a 1 or 2-year program abroad. In addition to providing desperately needed insight, managers would be gaining exposure to a potentially profitable market. American and Western European participants could be found both among recently retired executives and business school faculties and among active managers in corporations and consulting firms. Joint ventures provide yet another way in which Western firms can lend their expertise to the CIS.

Market Access and Restrictions on Technology. To provide a market for Russian goods and commodities, the United States and Western nations could move to dismantle barriers to their domestic markets that affect the former Soviet republics. Also, if CIS nations are to modernize both their industries and their society, they will need more advanced telecommunications and technology products. Currently, residual cold war regulations prohibit U.S. and other Western companies from exporting technology to, or investing in, Russia. The United States has taken hesitant steps in this direction already, but continuing to eliminate such restrictions would not only create opportunities for American companies but also help speed economic development in the CIS.

Direct Private Investment. The IMF estimates that the CIS will need almost $100 billion over the next four years, only $44 billion of which is likely to come from governments. The rest will come from the private sector if governments in the republics take steps to encourage capital investments and make private enterprise viable. U.S. business has the opportunity to gain early access to what could become one of the world's largest and most profitable markets. One of the top priorities for the architects of market economies in the CIS should be the removal of impediments to foreign investment or joint ventures with local companies.

THE COST OF SECURITY

Administering the aid package we have described will not be cheap. Neither Congress nor the Administration should pretend that securing freedom and laying the foundation for economic growth in the Commonwealth of Independent States can be achieved without cost to the United States. Even conservative estimates suggest that the United States must be ready to supply at least $3 billion a year in aid or standby credits. Nor, for that matter, will aid guarantee a smooth transition to democracy and a prosperous future for the citizens of the republics. As a nation, we must be realistic about both our costs and our expectations. We must also be swift and resolute in taking advantage of this opportunity.

The amount of aid needed is substantial, but it is inconsequential when compared with the trillions that we spent defending the nation during the Cold War. The United States should not let pressing domestic problems deter us from investing in our future security. **If we fail to cultivate a peaceful transition to democracy and the free market for the CIS and are forced to rearm in the future, we will have even fewer resources for our domestic needs.**

COOPERATION IN THE 1990s

Throughout the cold war, the threat of superpower conflict served as an organizing principle for international relations. From the conclusion of World War II until the early

---

PRIVATE SECTOR INVESTMENT IN THE CIS

Aid from official sources is expected to furnish less than half the capital necessary to transform the former Soviet republics into market economies. To make up the difference, planners are counting on an infusion of capital from international businesses. Although many Western corporations are eager to gain access to the rich natural resources and top scientific talent of the former Soviet Union, they face an array of challenges. Western attempts at investment or joint ventures have been stymied by a general fear of instability and a range of legal and logistical hazards.

Jurisdictional problems and obsolete regulations have constrained the ability of Western companies to operate in CIS nations. Tax agreements between Western corporations and CIS states can suddenly change and new taxes can be levied haphazardly. White Nights, a west Siberian joint venture equally owned by Varyeganneftygaz, a Russian production company, and a Western group made up of Houston-based Anglo-Suisse and New York-based Phibro Energy Inc., found that separate taxes to different government bodies absorbed almost all of their profits. Corporations doing business in the CIS often find that imports of necessary technologies and equipment are prohibited. Export opportunities are limited as well: because of an oil shortage of their own, Russians are wary of allowing foreigners to export oil for hard currency. Finally, rivalries between different power bases within the CIS can make investment by Western companies risky. Until jurisdictions are clarified and rational commercial laws enforced, operating in the former Soviet Union will continue to be a risky enterprise.

Despite the hazards, some Western companies have enthusiastically structured agreements to invest in the CIS states. In early March, 1992, Sun Microsystems, an American computer company, became one of the first Western companies to take advantage of the substantial technical and scientific talent within the CIS. Sun will work cooperatively with the scientist who created supercomputers for the Soviet military and space program, Boris A. Babayan. Babayan and his team of about 50 software and hardware designers have entered into a long-term research agreement with Sun to do joint research on SPARC, an advanced computer architecture. Babayan and his team will remain employees of the Moscow Institute, but will receive additional funding and computers from Sun. Sun will not discuss the business terms of the agreement in detail, but the Russian scientists will be paid far less than American computer designers who typically earn $100,000 a year or more. Other high technology companies, such as Apple Computer Inc. and Microsoft Corporation, are also searching for ways to tap the technical and scientific expertise within the CIS.

A private sector investment in the CIS of much greater magnitude is the agreement between Chevron Corporation and the former Soviet republic of Kazakhstan to jointly develop the Tengiz oil field, one of the largest oil fields in the world. The venture is expected to require a $20 billion investment over the life of the project. Chevron will likely invest up to $10 billion over the next 40 years, with an initial investment of $1.5 billion in the first three years. Industry sources expect the field to someday produce 700,000 barrels of oil a day and generate revenues of more than $5 billion a year. Chevron will have a 50% interest in the venture but Kazakhstan will get 80% of the income after Chevron pays taxes and royalties on its share.

The interest of Western companies in pursuing projects like these will increase greatly if the governments in these new nations reconfigure regulations which block or inhibit commercial activity. Since private capital will be critical to economic development in the CIS, official aid and technical assistance should place a high priority on removing these obstacles.

1970s, the United States, as the clear leader of the West, could substantially influence much of the international agenda. Until the end of the Cold War, concern over presenting a unified front against the Soviet threat served to dampen the economic conflicts that arose from growing interdependence. The demise of the Soviet Union has removed these restraints and unleashed disintegrative threats at a time when the potential gains from cooperation are the greatest. These disintegrative forces also have the potential to create ill effects worldwide.

We live in an era in which many of the most pressing issues that a country faces are international in scope. Economic growth and the spread of technology have given power to private, nonstate actors in international affairs. The source of these transnational problems is no longer some distant "evil empire." Often, problems rooted in our own societies flow across national borders. Factories emit pollutants into the air, health threats such as acquired immune deficiency syndrome (AIDS) cross national borders, and corporations sell military technologies to other nations. These spillovers impose costs that are beyond any individual country's control. It is in this context that a new strategy for cooperative effort gains importance.

Solving these issues will require international cooperation, which can often be hard to achieve. Endemic to all collaborative international efforts is the so-called free-rider problem. Addressing transnational issues often requires a large pool of resources. When contributions to this pool are voluntary, many nations fail to contribute fully because they will benefit no matter how great their commitment. During the cold war, some believed that America's allies underspent on their military needs because the United States provided for the Western defense. Without clear leadership in assigning costs, it is exceedingly difficult to marshal the resources needed to mount a successful international effort.

A unique aspect of the transnational problems created by individual actions is that private actors can easily cross national boundaries to escape laws or regulations they find onerous. The B.C.C.I. scandal was largely the result of bankers trying to escape regulation by moving funds between countries with different rules. More generally, a country that unilaterally enacts particularly strict regulations in any area ranging from the environment to financial services may find that its businesses are relocating to countries with a lesser regulatory burden. In the case of a country that enacts strict environmental regulations, the country will lose jobs, but the amount of pollution in the earth's atmosphere will stay about the same. This dynamic gives countries very little incentive to attack such problems unilaterally.

In some instances, military force or other traditional instruments of power may help to solve problems; however, they will generally be insufficient. International agreements, such as the 1987 Montreal Protocol Agreement that phased out the production of chloroflourocarbons (CFCs), that bind nations to change domestic policies can solve some problems. In areas such as terrorism and drug trafficking, information sharing may be useful. Punitive actions, such as political nonrecognition and trade bans, to isolate countries that serve as havens for terrorists and drug producers may also be effective. We have laid much of the groundwork necessary to deal with these new global issues, but to successfully address the range of new challenges, **the United States will need to expand its commitment to, and reliance on, collaborative international effort.[6] With our unique national capabilities, American effort can both strengthen and promote the use of international negotiation to confront the new problems facing the world.**

In the post cold war environment, it will be increasingly important for countries to cooperate. But without an immediate security threat, real and sustained collaboration will be hard to achieve. Nations are likely to perceive various issues quite differently, making it difficult to define the common interest. Given its leadership role during the cold war and its continuing military dominance, the United States may be tempted to define the common interest unilaterally and then demand that others share in its cost. Although the United States still must be able to defend its own interests, drastic U.S. action is likely to antagonize our allies. **If the United States wants the other nations of the world to share the costs of cooperative efforts, it will have to be more willing to use international institutions and to share decision making power**. For example, although Germany and Japan will both be expected to assume larger burdens in the 1990s, neither country is currently a permanent member of the U.N. Security Council. As one observer put it, "While others were free riders [during the cold war], the Americans had full control of the steering wheel. If others pay a fare, they will have a greater say about where the bus will go."[7]

Powerful third parties necessitate a greater reliance on international institutions that coordinate collaborative action. There are five main ways that these institutions facilitate cooperation: (1) providing a formalized manner of sharing costs (2) establishing standards and procedures for consultation (3) increasing the amount of information available to nations (4) creating incentives for countries to bargain in good faith and (5) allowing countries to influence and react to each others domestic policies.[8]

In this new environment, however, multilateral organizations will be asked to assume new roles. Increasingly, countries will want to have more to say about each other's domestic policies. Past topics for international negotiation included the distribution of defense costs and the level of a country's tariffs, but new issues will strike much more at national sovereignty. The current U.S. contention that European countries should reduce farm subsidies is an example of this type of disagreement. To balance the need to consider the international effects of domestic policies with the right of national sovereignty, multilateral organizations will have to establish a framework for negotiation. The attempt to strengthen the dispute mechanisms in GATT through the Uruguay Round is a real example of a multilateral organization grappling with this very issue. The world community will need to continually assess the ability of each of the multilateral organizations to accomplish its goals and to adapt to new challenges.

In this new cooperative framework, the People's Republic of China stands out as a special case. Its size (it is home to nearly one-fifth of the world's people), burgeoning economic power, and military might make it necessary that China be a participant in addressing the problems outlined above. But its role in these efforts has yet to be defined. Recent economic liberalization has brought about greater contact with the outside world; it now seeks a greater role in international organizations, such as membership in GATT, and has signed on to two weapons treaties in the past year. Even U.S. companies have begun to benefit from economic relationships with China. These are indeed hopeful signs. But at the same time, its history of human rights abuses and suspected contribution to weapons proliferation have engendered resentment and fear in the community of nations. In addition, chronic trade imbalances with industrial countries (in particular, the United States) threaten to limit its access to international markets. While China's increased contact with the world is a positive sign, policy towards China needs to ensure that the ongoing economic liberalization brings about political reform. Without Chinese participation, many of the most pressing problems confronting the world will go largely unresolved.

In the 1990s, it will be vital for the international community to cooperate on both the more traditional transnational issues and the newer ones that result from private action. This policy statement will concentrate on those economic issues that require concerted efforts at cooperation. We do not suggest that they will be the only areas of cooperation in the 1990s. The three transnational economic issues to which the United States should give priority and should press ahead to develop a collective agenda for are: international trade and investment, healthy global economic growth, and integration of the developing world into the global economy. (For a detailed discussion see Chapter 3). Success in these areas will affect other objectives and promote the well-being of people worldwide.

THE UNITED STATES AS THE RALLIER OF NATIONS

Although the new model for relationships between countries will be based on cooperative agreement and shared burdens, there will still be a pressing need for active and effective world leadership, redefined to meet new challenges. Leadership will require making a persuasive case for a collective agenda among nations and using a broad range of economic, strategic, and political tools to spur international action in addressing this agenda. The international leader in this new global age will not be a nation that uses force to achieve its own goals but a rallier of nations, capable of making divergent countries see a commonality of interests and motivating them to act.

The United States, with its exceptional military power and its lack of territorial or ideological ambitions, its traditions of tolerance, and its inherent economic, political, and cultural strengths, is uniquely qualified to provide leadership in the efforts of an interdependent world community. Within the framework of protected cooperative effort, U.S. leadership should seek to identify a shared set of goals among divergent national interests. These shared goals could then serve as a collective agenda for international action

---

ENVIRONMENTAL ISSUES AND THE NEED FOR GLOBAL COOPERATION

Environmental issues are not new to the international agenda. Pollution moving across national frontiers has long been a serious irritant in relations between bordering nations; some have even likened it to military attacks.

Diplomatic efforts to cope with pollution have, however, yielded some promising results. International accords of recent years, including agreements to reduce acid rain and prevent further damage to the ozone layer, provide models for future action on an increasing array of international environmental concerns.

There is now potential for a much more complex environmental problem: global climate change. The available scientific evidence has fostered disagreement on whether continued buildup of greenhouse gases in the atmosphere will increase average global temperatures and what the effects of a rise in temperatures would be on the quality of human life. Many believe, with some confidence, that any effects on incomes and health will not be felt uniformly across the globe.

TRANSBOUNDARY POLLUTION

Pollution crosses national boundaries in several ways: acid deposition, river and ocean pollution, and as demonstrated by the Chernobyl disaster, nuclear fallout.

About half of the air pollutants in European countries originate in other European countries. About half of Canada's acid rain derives from emissions in the United States, while approximately 20 percent of the United States' acid rain is thought to result from Canadian emissions. How energy is used and wastes are disposed of in one country must concern neighboring nations. Not only is human health at risk from pollution from neighboring states, but damage to waterways and forests will create economic hardships and jeopardize valuable recreational and ecological resources. With respect to global climate change and stratospheric ozone depletion, the effects are global and require global solutions.

Treaties resulting from ad hoc diplomatic negotiations have been the customary means of dealing with international environmental issues. Except where only a few countries with comparable wealth are involved, such treaties have avoided commitments for specific actions. When numerous countries involved have differing economic and public health interests in an environmental problem, it has been difficult to achieve real change.

The *1987 Montreal Protocol on Substances That Deplete the Ozone Layer*, concluded after the scientific evidence of the ozone phenomenon was understood, provides the most useful precedent for an agreement governing global climate change. Parties to the 1987 agreement undertook specific commitments to phase out production of ozone-depleting substances. The protocol recognized that countries have different needs and capabilities. Developing countries were given ten years longer to comply, and a multilateral fund was established to facilitate financial and technical assistance to those countries.

through the appropriate international institutions or set of nations. The United States is still the only nation that possesses the range of tangible and intangible qualities needed to assume the role as a rallier of nations.

While possessing the traditional prerequisites for international leadership — military might, a large and diverse national economy, abundant natural resources — the United States also has leadership attributes uniquely important in this new world: Our language and culture have become nearly universal and English is now unquestionably the language of international commerce. America's tradition of assimilating and drawing economic strength from immigrants and a diverse population will be a unique advantage. And in a technological world, where knowledge is a critical asset, the United States remains the preeminent scientific power.

ACHIEVEMENTS OF AMERICAN LEADERSHIP

American leadership has already played a vital role in helping to bring about a more secure and prosperous world. Despite the residual threats discussed earlier, American leadership during the cold war helped to free the people of Eastern Europe and the Soviet Union itself from the yoke of communism. The

---

GLOBAL CLIMATE CHANGE

We also regard multilateral negotiations as the only realistic approach if the threat of global climate change warrants significant political action. The incentive for action by individual nations is often weak because the benefits may accrue largely to others. In addition, actions by a single country to reduce emissions of greenhouse gases will not have a large impact on the global-warming threat.

Poorer countries, which tend to be more heavily reliant on climate-sensitive industries such as agriculture, forestry, and grazing, are threatened with the most severe repercussions from climate change. These countries can least afford the technology required to adjust their energy use and so reduce atmospheric levels of carbon dioxide and other greenhouse gases.

Many countries wish to move more quickly than does the United States to reduce emissions of carbon dioxide, one of the greenhouse gases, even though scientific evidence of its relationship to global warming is inconclusive and probably will remain so for at least another decade. The United States, which is the world's largest consumer of coal (22 percent), oil (25 percent), and natural gas (28 percent), and which emits about 20 percent of man-made carbon dioxide, will therefore be put under pressure to shoulder a considerable portion of the burden, probably through a combination of drastically reduced consumption of fossil fuels and provision of financial and technical assistance to developing countries for improvements in energy efficiency. Without such assistance from the wealthier countries, the developing countries will have a strong disincentive to sign any agreement to reduce emissions.

In principle, international collaboration might greatly reduce the total worldwide cost of attacking global climate change. Reductions in greenhouse emissions have approximately the same effect on the climate wherever they originate. However, it is often more costly to achieve additional reductions in emissions in advanced countries where substantial reduction efforts have already been undertaken than in lower-income countries where technology lags and no such efforts have been made. Thus, advanced industrial countries may find it cheaper to achieve their share of improved climate in less developed countries rather than at home. For example, if an American electric power company were required to reduce carbon dioxide emissions by a given tonnage, it could do this at a much smaller cost by subsidizing such reductions in India or China. The net cost would be less, and the earth's environment would still benefit substantially. Because of these possibilities, an international cooperative approach to global climate change has special advantages. Moreover, because of the size of the U.S. economy and the high level of energy use, American leverage will be vital to enacting and enforcing meaningful international environmental agreements.

threat of nuclear war between the superpowers, which had long haunted the world, appears to be a thing of the past. These achievements would not have been possible without the resources and strategic perseverance of the United States over a span of four decades.

Also, early U.S. support for global economic institutions, such as the United Nations, the GATT system, the World Bank, the IMF, and the OECD, was essential to the development of the current world economy. Through these institutions, the United States was able to galvanize much of the industrial world with its stress on the benefits of open markets worldwide and fair treatment for international commerce. In addition to promoting economic integration, The United Nations has recently become a more powerful force for countering aggression and advancing political stability.

Recently, the United States has neglected many of its commitments to these institutions, shirking some financial responsibilities and failing to exert the institutional leadership demanded by changing times. Only the United States, using access to its vast internal market, its military power, its giant capital base, and its intangible leadership qualities as tools, can exercise the leadership necessary to reshape these institutions to meet current challenges. And as a leader, we must be prepared to shoulder our fair share of the financial burden. Paying our share is not only wise; it is cost-effective. **Having invested trillions of dollars and thousands of American lives to win the cold war, we should be willing to make a relatively small investment in our ability to further the causes of peace and cooperation among nations**. Agile American diplomacy will also be central to this effort; we should not fail to provide the diplomatic resources needed to build and manage these cooperative efforts.

Making good on our commitments to these organizations is an important first step, but it is not enough. America must urge other nations to increase their commitment to, and reliance on, the United Nations, the World Bank, and the IMF. Most important, to ensure that other nations are willing to expand their international commitments, we must be willing to share not only the financial burdens but also the leadership. We cannot expect our partners to assume greater responsibility for the costs of international cooperation without giving them a more substantial voice in how their money is spent, even if this means yielding some U.S. control. As we increase our demands on these institutions we need to also focus on refitting them to more effectively fulfill their missions.

THE CHANGING FOUNDATIONS OF AMERICAN WORLD LEADERSHIP

Can the United States rally its own people to adapt to the leadership challenges of a new world? Some skeptics of America's ability to maintain a world leadership role argue that the United States is in decline because of excessive global ambitions and overspending for military and foreign policy purposes in the effort to maintain global dominance. This international focus, coupled with underinvestment at home, has served to weaken the nation's economic and social foundations. The evidence to support this thesis includes the United States' sluggish productivity growth and our transformation from being the world's largest creditor nation into the world's largest debtor.

We find this "declinist" thesis unduly fatalistic; it greatly underestimates America's residual strengths. The United States' outstanding strength is probably its resilience: the resilience it demonstrated when it swiftly emerged from the Depression of the 1930s to become the arsenal of democracy and leader of the free world and, when the war was won, to lead the reconstruction of the economies of both its allies and its former enemies. Indeed, some of the evidence adduced to show American decline is essentially a consequence of America's deliberate policy of aiding world reconstruction after the Second World War.

In truth, the United States must maintain an active and visible presence in world affairs. **U.S. economic growth and continuing improvement in the quality of American life depend on our economic relationships with other nations; they are markets for products, sources for capital and ideas, and competitors forcing U.S. enterprise to excel**. Failure to lead in the process of continuing integration could harm the United States in two ways. U.S. businesses could find themselves shut out of international markets by unfair foreign policies or hamstrung by anachronistic domestic regulation, and renewed threats to national security would require diverting money from productive use to military use.

A commitment to an open global economy does not mean that U.S. policy makers can be indifferent to product and capital flows. Although, in technical terms, invested capital can earn returns anywhere in the world, U.S. policy makers have a large stake in ensuring that capital, both U.S. and foreign, is invested here. When goods and services are produced abroad, U.S. investors benefit; but when high value-added goods and services are produced here, both American workers and American investors benefit.

Some have argued that trying to slow or even stop the integration of the global economy is the best means of keeping American living standards high. In fact, trying to forestall integration will only damage American prospects for economic growth and a rising standard of living for all Americans. Cutting our ties to the global economy will limit American businesses to a slowly growing domestic market and would deprive the United States of welcome foreign capital and the jobs it creates. **The interests of current and future American workers are best served by making the United States an attractive place to produce goods and services.** We can achieve this by investing in our human capital, building a better system of public and technical infrastructure, and ensuring that workers displaced by shifts in global commerce are effectively retrained so that they can contribute to the economy again.

The United States' relative decline is unquestionably a matter for serious concern. Yet, it needs to be understood in historical context. Some decline in relative productivity, living standards, and technological development resulted from the economic convergence of the industrial countries of the West, as capital and technology were transferred from the leader, the United States, to other countries.

The high level of U.S. military spending played a crucial role in the containment of Soviet expansion and, finally, in the end of the cold war; but even though the United States has carried a heavier military burden than its allies, proportionately as well as absolutely, **there is little or no reason to conclude that America's economic weaknesses stem from excessive military spending**. American expenditures on military objectives in recent years have been proportionately far lower than they were in earlier periods.

Figure 4 demonstrates, shortly before World War II broke out, America was producing about one-fourth of total world output; under the special conditions of the war and early postwar period, when other countries' economies were devastated, the United States' share of world output rose to slightly more than one-third. But as other industrial countries recovered, the American share of world output gradually fell back to about its pre World War II level of approximately one-fourth and stayed there until 1989.[9]

But there are now grounds for concern that after stabilizing between 1970 to 1987, America's rate of economic growth may be slipping again, jeopardizing our position of

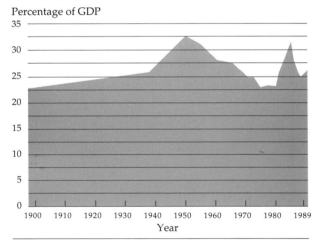

Figure 4

U.S. Share of World Production
1900-1989

Percentage of GDP

SOURCE: Herbert Block, *The Planetary Product in 1980: A Creative Pause?* (Washington, D.C.: U.S. Dept. of State, Bureau of Public Affairs, 1981), pp. 74-77, 86-87; Simon Kuznets, *Economic Growth and Structure* (New York: W.W. Norton, 1965), p. 144; United Nations, private correspondence.

global leadership in the economic age. The two most significant areas that the United States must address if it is to maintain its position of global leadership are investment in physical capital and technology and the quality of our future human resources.

The decline in American investment in capital goods, infrastructure, research, and education during the past decade will almost inevitably cause a sharp future decline of the U.S. share of world production. Unless there is a rise from the very low level of U.S. domestic saving, the level of domestic investment will remain unacceptably low; the drag of inadequate saving can be relieved only by cutting the public-sector deficit and increasing the rate of private saving. This and other macroeconomic strategies for boosting our competitive position are spelled out more fully in Chapter 3.

Also of great concern is the failure of the American work force to keep pace with the demands of astounding technological change. To build the skills of our future work force, the United States needs a comprehensive human-investment strategy, as outlined in Chapter 4, to enable all Americans, especially the disadvantaged, to productively participate in and enjoy the rewards of the mainstream economy. Unless we place a high priority on extending the American dream to all Americans, we risk losing the moral stature that is so important in motivating and inspiring other nations.

America is not guaranteed a position of effective world leadership. If we are to lead, we must redeploy our resources in the interests of both peace and prosperity. In the world that is emerging, economic growth will be a greater guarantor of peace than military might. America's leadership will be crucial to preserve and expand the open world economy that gave all free nations a long spell of growth, unprecedented in history.

DIRECTIONS FOR POLICY

1. Although the new model for relationships between countries will be based on cooperative agreement and shared burdens, there will still be a pressing need for active and effective world leadership. With its vast political, cultural, and military resources, the United States is uniquely qualified for the role as a rallier of nations, able to motivate others to act for the common good.

2. Issues such as environmental pollution, terrorism, and weapons proliferation will be impossible to solve without collaborative international efforts. As a rallier of nations, the United States should place a high priority on building cooperative efforts to address security and other concerns. International organizations will be critical to achieving these goals. Past American support has helped create global institutions such as the United Nations, GATT, and the World Bank; future American leadership will be necessary to help these and other organizations to meet new challenges.

3. The United States has a critical role to play in ensuring the transition from autocracy to democracy in the former Soviet Union. U.S. aid will be crucial in facilitating internal reforms and helping to deter political instability. The U.S. should be prepared to spend at least $3 billion a year in aid or standby credits. In order to ensure that the aid is well-spent, the U.S. must work in accord with other supranational organizations to foster political stability and economic development in the region.

CHAPTER 3

LEADERSHIP IN INTERNATIONAL ECONOMIC COOPERATION

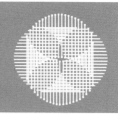

A U.S. global economic strategy needs to have a clear set of objectives. Three critical priorities for international cooperation will require vigorous American leadership in the coming years.

First, all countries need access to world markets to enjoy the benefits of economic growth. After the most rapid expansion of world trade in history, support for the open world trading system is eroding as a result of recession, unemployment, industrial overcapacity in some industries, and rising nationalism. The open world economy is in danger of splitting into hostile and protectionist trading blocs. If this trend continues, a breakdown in world trade could produce an economic and political disaster of the kind that took place at the start of the Great Depression. And yet, for the first time in history, billions of people worldwide, in the formerly communist countries and in the developing world, are clamoring to be admitted to the world trading system, even as some industrial nations fail to recognize its benefits. To prevent such a breakdown in trade from occurring, the United States should continue defending the existing system of world trade and should work to broaden and deepen it. The continued growth of the world economy depends on including new countries and on facilitating international investment and trade in manufactured and agricultural products, financial and other services, and intellectual property. This will require breaking down the barriers to trade and countering unfair trading practices that some countries still pursue.

Second, the growth and stability of the world economy will require cooperation in macroeconomic policy among the major industrial countries. It will also require cooperation in building a more stable exchange rate system to keep trade and investment flowing freely. The United States, while working for world economic growth and integration, has itself been a source of currency disorders and trade and payments imbalances stemming in part from its chronic budget deficits. These fiscal deficits have aggravated its external deficits and have reduced U.S. savings, investment, and growth. For its own economic health and that of the world economy, the United States should set medium-term targets to raise national saving and achieve a surplus in the federal budget within a decade. With such policies in place, the United States would have more credibility to encourage other countries to reduce budget deficits and increase the world supply of capital needed to promote stronger growth in the industrial countries, the developing countries, and the new states emerging from communism.

Third, the end of superpower rivalry gives America and its partners a chance to foster economic growth and alleviate the severe poverty that afflicts the developing world. The plight of these nations will become even more important as they experience unprecedented population growth in the years ahead.

A. INTERNATIONAL TRADE AND INVESTMENT[1]

Just as market-driven national economies have demonstrated their superiority over centrally planned and rigidly controlled economies, the liberalization of international trade and investment has proven its advantages over protected systems. The movement toward more open world markets has greatly enhanced the efficiency of the world economy. Since the end of World War II, the United States has actively pressed for open markets. It has taken this position not only to promote its own interests but to work for the benefit of the world as a whole, especially the developing world.

As a result, in the last two decades, trade, capital flows, investment, and output have grown at historically unprecedented rates, as nations and industries benefited from economies of scale, increased competition, and a more rational deployment of resources. World exports grew from $290 billion in 1970 to more than $2,910 billion in 1990, or nearly twice as fast as the expansion of world output. Most significantly, the international flow of capital, which has financed the expanding world economy, has seen the most explosive growth. Deposit banks' foreign assets, one measure of capital flows, skyrocketed from $160 billion in 1970 to $6,780 billion in 1989, or at a rate six times as fast as world output (Figure 5). Foreign direct investment has also outpaced world output.

Despite the importance of this dynamic, neither the economic successes of some nations nor the failures of others can be ascribed simply to the more open world economy. A liberal trade and investment system is a necessary but not a sufficient condition for the growth and prosperity of nations. Even more important are the responses of individual nations to the opportunities offered by a more open world economic order. Nations may grasp the opportunities to capitalize on export-led growth or spoil their chances through inappropriate fiscal and monetary policies. By creating inflation and distorting resource use, such policies disrupt the production of goods and services. In addition, protectionist policies, excessive government subsidies to special-interest groups, and

Figure 5

World GDP, World Exports, and Deposit Banks' Foreign Assets
1970-1991

Trillions of Current U.S. Dollars, Log Scale

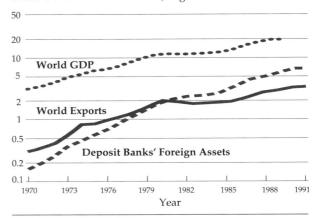

SOURCE: World GDP: UN personal correspondence; World Exports: United Nations Handbook of International Trade and Development Statisitics, 1980 & 1990 Suppl.; 1989 International Trade Statisitics Yearbook, Volume 1; Deposit Bank Foreign Assets: IMF International Financial Statistics; personal correspondence.

NOTE: While GDP and export data include CIS and Eastern European countries, data on Deposit Banks' Foreign Assets does not.

undue regulation of business activity reduce productive efficiency, misdirect national resources, and breed corruption. Similarly, a nation that saves too little and invests too little in its physical and human resources can never realize the full benefits of an open world economy.

UNFAIR TRADE: SHORT-TERM AND MEDIUM-TERM APPROACHES

Private businesses adapt to the global economy more naturally and readily than governments. Businesses, subject to intense international competition, benefit from a worldwide flow of capital and technology. Politicians, on the other hand, seek votes only from their national or local constituencies: As Tip O'Neill, former Speaker of the United States House of Representatives, once said, "All politics is local."

In times of recession or depression, support for open trade often weakens, not only among business groups but also among labor and the community generally, as nations turn inward and citizens fear economic change. During the four decades after World War II, self-interested behavior was held in check by the commonly perceived threat of Soviet aggression. As that fear has receded, cohesion among the advanced industrial countries is eroding, and countries feel freer to pursue national and regional arrangements in the mistaken assumption that such actions best protect their home and regional markets.

Too many business executives and workers, and even some economists, regard the arguments in favor of an open trading system as unrealistic and obsolete in a world where the spread of capital and technology may swiftly undermine a nation's comparative advantage. Their doubts are strengthened when foreign competitors benefit from the contrived comparative advantage resulting from government subsidies or resort to predatory means of taking over domestic or third-country markets. These practices have prompted increasing calls for aggressive bilateral trade policies, some of which border on protectionism.

Some nations today pursue a policy closely akin to eighteenth-century mercantilism, seeking to amass foreign assets by subsidizing exports and blocking imports, thereby creating a trade surplus. Those who advocate more aggressive bilateral measures, recognizing the danger of provoking retaliation, often call for "managed trade," by which they mean quotas or other arrangements for market sharing or cartelization of trade on a bilateral or multilateral basis. This, they contend, is necessary to prevent economic disorder in a time of excess world capacity.

And some critics maintain that the liberal traders have not developed a satisfactory strategy for dealing with those countries that engage in unfair practices and open or covert discrimination, threatening the existence of producers whose markets are open to foreign penetration without gaining equal access to foreign markets.

Some advocates of liberal trade argue that "dumping"—selling goods abroad below their home production costs and prices—and export subsidies could be ignored because they provided benefits to consumers in the short run and would disappear in the longer run as unprofitable. But that argument has not convinced injured producers and workers or even some consumers, who fear that once the foreign predator has put the domestic producers out of business, it will exploit its monopoly and raise prices; and that once it gains the advantage of large-scale production and confronts would-be competitors with the high costs of getting back into the market, the predator will make it impossible for domestic producers to regain market share. Even if these fears are exaggerated, political pressures for protectionism may become too powerful to resist unless trade is perceived as not only free but fair.

Unfair trade can arise not only from the subsidization and dumping of foreign products into the U.S. market but also from formal or informal restrictions on access to foreign markets. Section 301 of the Trade Act of 1974 empowers the President to act against such practices when they are determined to be unjustifiable, unreasonable, or discriminatory to U.S. producers. The logic behind Section 301 is that access to the vast U.S. domestic market should be used as a lever to open markets abroad.

Section 301 has been criticized as excessively unilateral in its determination procedure and as relying on the threat of retaliation that might escalate into a cycle of counter-retaliation. In its actual application, however, the United States has exercised restraint; for example, only six Section 301 investigations were initiated in 1991, and not one threat of counter-protectionism has materialized. Not only has a cycle of counterretaliation been avoided, but in a number of cases the use of 301 has strengthened the multilateral system by opening markets for all countries, not just the United States.

The issue of fair trade has arisen most sharply with respect to Japan. In its drive for rapid economic growth, the government of Japan has singled out particular industries for government support through various forms of subsidy and/or protection in their early stages. In some cases, the subsidies have taken the form of outright grants or preferential credits, and the targeted industries have often benefited from the indirect subsidization created by protection from imports. As these industries matured, some firms kept their prices high in their protected home markets and used the excess profits to sell some of their products at a lower price in the United States and other nations. This strategy has put severe competitive pressure on U.S. firms and enabled some Japanese firms to move quickly up the learning curve, expand, and realize economies of scale. As the Japanese firms achieved success not only domestically but also in the world market, the Japanese government progressively reduced the subsidies and lifted the protection.

Such government support has not been the only reason for the competitive success of certain Japanese industries (and in many cases it has played a very small role). A highly competitive domestic market and sound, long-term investment strategies by Japanese managers have also contributed to Japanese success.

To counter the adverse competitive effects of such foreign industrial policies, should the United States do likewise? Should the government identify sectors of the U.S. economy that hold particular promise for growth, especially high-technology industries — and nurture their growth?

Business advocates of a U.S. industrial policy have been bolstered in recent years by academic literature setting forth what has come to be called "strategic trade policy." Advocates base their case for government support of particular industries on the need to offset two types of market failure in modern industrial economies: externalities and monopoly profits. *Externalities* are benefits of productive activity that accrue to parties outside the firm. In high-technology industries, firms invest heavily in research and development, take high risks, and often incur initial losses in developing new products. However, the full benefits of investment in new knowledge cannot be captured by the firm incurring the cost because some of the gains spill over to other firms able to imitate the techniques of the leaders. Strategic trade theorists argue that government intervention is legitimate in industries that generate substantial external benefits.

The second type of market failure that is claimed to justify an industrial policy is the absence of perfect competition in some sectors. In industries characterized by increasing returns to scale, only a few large firms may be in effective competition. Under such conditions, excess profits are generated by firms that compete internationally. Champions of industrial policy argue that the national interest will be served by subsidizing those industries to shift the excess returns from foreign to domestic firms, thereby raising national income at the expense of other countries.

Nevertheless, even some leading students of strategic trade theory acknowledge that however compelling the theoretical case for industrial targeting may appear to be, it would be unlikely to work in practice in the United States.[2] How would the strategic industries be identified? Political influence by industries seeking government help, or favor-granting by politicians seeking electoral or financial support, would commonly be determining factors, and selective intervention would fall prey to pork-barrel politics. It is unlikely, at best, that bureaucratic allocation of resources to particular industries would be more effective than decision making by business executives and investors in response to the interplay of market forces. Subsidizing some industries would hurt other industries by drawing resources away from them. Managed trade also tends to defer adjustment to foreign competition by industries and makes adjustment more difficult and extreme when it finally comes. As we are seeing in Eastern Europe and the former Soviet Union, it is better to have a process of continuing adjustments than suppression followed by a big bang. Finally, there would be the risk of foreign retaliation to actions that could hurt many of our trading partners and violate trade rules under GATT that the United States has long supported.

Rather than adopting the predatory practices of other nations or engaging in industrial policy or managed trade, the United States should vigorously counter such practices. To the maximum extent possible, this should be done through the GATT remedial process. Where that option is unavailable or too slow and cumbersome, we should be prepared to aggressively use our own unfair trade statutes (such as Section 301) to open foreign

markets, to discourage unfair penetration of our domestic market through dumping and subsidization, and to deter the infringement of intellectual property rights. The U.S. has been slow to act aggressively in this area. However, we should limit the definition of dumping to selling in foreign markets at lower prices than at home and halt the tendency of recent years to resort to the unfair trade laws as instruments of outright protection.

New rules should be developed to provide more effective remedies for the adverse effects of governments that target particular domestic industries for special assistance and support. Current countervailing remedies are inadequate; the damage to competing industries in other countries may not occur for a number of years, by which time the subsidization will have been withdrawn. Moreover, there may be no quantitative link, as assumed

---

THE UNITED STATES AND JAPAN

The economic and political relationship of the United States and Japan has come under much scrutiny in recent years, as the security concerns which had governed international relations have been diminished by the collapse of the Soviet Union. The often harmful political rhetoric on both sides of the Pacific tends to obscure two important components of the issue: The economic health of each nation is largely dependent on the other and the political relationship between the two nations will be essential to fostering any sort of cooperation on global issues. A deterioration in either the economic or political relationship between these nations would have detrimental effects for the citizens of both countries and the world economy as whole.

Both the U.S. and Japanese economies would suffer if economic relations were to sour. Japan's export-oriented economy relies heavily on United States markets. Japanese exports to the United States represent 29% of its GDP. Recent measures by the European Community to restrict Japanese market access, coupled with the small size of the East Asian market, underscore the need for Japanese industry to have access to the vast U.S. market. At the same time, the United States has a significant economic interest in maintaining close ties to Japan. As the second-largest direct foreign investor in the United States, Japan plays a significant role in creating American jobs. Japan is also the second largest market in the world. The rate of annual direct foreign investment in Japan has doubled, from $2.2 billion in 1987 to $4.3 billion in 1991. Despite some signs of liberalizing access to its market and encouraging direct foreign investment, Japan's chronic trade surpluses and limits on foreign investment have strained relations with the United States.

Besides their mutual economic interests, the United States and Japan have global economic and political interests; in a world where economic power is of primary importance, these two nations are responsible for one third of world GNP. This economic might translates into a substantial stake in international organizations. The United States and Japan are, respectively, the largest and second largest contributors to the United Nations and the IMF. The size of their economies also should enable them to exert considerable influence over GATT, although Japan seems hesitant to exercise this power. Deployed in the interest of furthering economic integration, this economic power could be a powerful force in cultivating agreement among nations.

Because the relationship between the two nations is of such importance, not only to the United States and Japan, but to other nations of the world, both nations need to address current sources of friction with real dialogue and action. In 1989, CED and its Japanese counterpart, Keizai Doyukai (the Japan Association of Corporate Executives), published a joint report entitled *Strengthening U.S. Japan Economic Relations: An Action Program for the Public and Private Sectors* which advocated the following steps to strengthen the relationship:

- The Japanese government needs to redesign policies which serve as regulatory barriers to imports and limit distribution of foreign products. The U.S. government should aim to eliminate the federal budget deficit and remove tax policies that encourage spending. Both governments should avoid unilateral trade restrictions.

- Japanese companies should cultivate more American suppliers and open up the closed elements of the Japanese business system; American business should tailor products to the Japanese market.

in the countervailing-duty concept, between the amount of the original subsidy and the extent of the current injury. High on the agenda of future trade negotiations should be revision of the GATT rules to address this problem.

ADJUSTING TO CHANGE

Because research and development does generate externalities in the sense of higher social returns than can be captured by the innovating firm, there is a strong case for partial government subsidy for such activity. This could be accomplished, without targeting individual industries, through an enhanced across-the-board tax credit for both basic and commercial research. Any U.S. government support for research and development should be available on equal terms to foreign-owned firms in the U.S., provided that their home countries are similarly open to direct investment from abroad and afford reciprocal access to research and development support for foreign firms operating in their jurisdictions. (Chapter 4 discusses this recommendation in greater detail.)

Proponents of managed trade argue that traditional supporters of open markets ignore the distributional effects of liberal trade on nations that lose industries and working people who lose jobs. That some industries in a country wind up big winners while others become big losers, say the proponents of managed trade, does not cancel out the distributional damages of open markets when labor or physical capital is not completely mobile.

Free-trade theorists respond that if the winners compensate the losers, there will be net gains to the nation as a whole. Some contend that the solution to this problem is to redistribute winners' gain among all citizens. However, if displaced workers lack the necessary education or training to move to the better-paid, higher-productivity jobs resulting from distributional change, they will suffer permanent losses. Unemployment benefits or welfare payments will not make them whole economically or restore the sense of worth that is closely linked to one's productive role in society. Indeed, the largest group of potential losers from the changing global distribution of industry may be relatively unskilled workers in the United States and other advanced-countries whose wages are under strong downward pressure as a result of competition with foreign firms using cheaper unskilled labor.

CED believes that income redistribution programs to counter the adverse effects of trade on some groups are not sound policy. Rather, gains from economic change should be used to finance public investments that will raise productivity and broaden opportunity for all our citizens. The best solution is to improve the education, skills, and mobility of all workers, especially the disadvantaged and displaced, to enable them to find new jobs and to adapt more flexibly to the demands of a rapidly changing and more integrated global economy.[3] Such programs will guarantee a more prosperous society for current and future Americans.

From a U.S. perspective, unfair trade practices are those actions by foreign companies or governments that reduce the international competitiveness of U.S. products or services in violation of the letter or spirit of international law. However, a number of serious impediments to the ability of U.S. firms to compete in the international marketplace stem from *domestic* laws and regulations. In effect, self-inflicted disadvantages can be considered unfair trade practices. Such disadvantages are found in a number of areas including strategic export controls, antitrust law, the Foreign Corrupt Practices Act, product liability law, and tax legislation. Reforms in these fields would also improve U.S. international competitiveness.

LONG-TERM BARRIERS TO TRADE AND INVESTMENT

The Uruguay Round of GATT negotiations has been the most complex and far-reaching set of trade negotiations ever undertaken. After six years of meetings, its outlook is still uncertain. On a few key issues, some nations remain more responsive to vocal domestic constituencies that would be hurt by an agreement than to the promise of greater long-run economic growth.

To its credit, the United States has been the most active advocate of a strong conclusion to the Round. Though guilty of some protectionist policies, the United States, far more than any of the other industrialized countries, is working to open the protected textile and agricultural markets of the world. With Europe seemingly preoccupied with its own political and economic union and Japan still reluctant to play a leadership role, even though it significantly benefits from open trade, the United States must continue its efforts at liberalization.

If the negotiations should fail, however, protectionist pressures both in the U.S. and abroad are likely to gather steam. Moreover, a unique opportunity to reduce the potentially trade-diverting effects of either the North American Free Trade Agreement (NAFTA), recently negotiated by the United States, Canada, and Mexico, and the current enlargement and deepening of the EC through multilateral liberalization will have been missed. In the absence of ongoing efforts to liberalize trade on a multilateral basis, the appeal of managed trade and bilateral and other discriminatory arrangements will increase. If the negotiations fail, these sub-GATT agreements could help to build momentum for another attempt at a multilateral agreement. In these circumstances, the United States should assert its role as rallier of nations to preserve the gains in liberalization already achieved in the seven previous GATT Rounds as a basis for a new collective effort when global conditions are more propitious.

If the Uruguay Round can be brought to a successful conclusion, it will be a tribute to U.S. efforts to bring about a more integrated global economic system by lowering or eliminating border restrictions to trade. The next and more difficult stage of integration will require that nations address more of the internal regulations and structural differences that are now the principal impediments to the further expansion of international trade and investment and the growth of world output.

The need to begin this transition to deeper integration has been recognized in both the Tokyo and Uruguay Rounds in negotiations over such matters as domestic subsidies, government procurement, health and safety standards, and the protection of intellectual property rights.

The sequence from shallow to deeper integration can be clearly discerned in the progress of the European Community. Originally concerned with eliminating border barriers and establishing a common external tariff, the EC realized it could not achieve a truly integrated market without harmonization and reduction of internal regulatory, structural, and institutional differences among member states. Hence, the Community adopted the Single European Act in 1986, with the objective of completing integration of the European internal market by the end of 1992. The aim of this far-reaching initiative is to harmonize rules on the establishment of businesses, product and environmental certification, tax policy, and labor relations. The goal for the year 2000 is to create a single European currency and central bank. This agreement must also resist the temptation to raise barriers to the rest of the world and thus be consistent with the GATT and the openness of the Uruguay Round. The recent difficulties that the EC has had in gaining individual national support for the Maastricht agreements illustrate how contentious an issue achieving deeper economic integration can be. Also, as the EC has tackled these issues, some leaders, calling such efforts necessarily anti-competitive and bureaucratic, have questioned the desirability of political and economic harmonization of such depth.

On a bilateral basis, the United States has also begun to address the effects on trade of domestic policies. The Structural Impediments Initiative (SII) discussions with Japan were aimed at reforming certain regulatory and structural aspects of the two economies believed to impede trade and balance-of-payments adjustment. On the Japanese side, the focus has been on such matters as domestic competition, including the reform of the keiretsu (an interlocking system of corporate ownership and supplier channels), deregulation of the distribution system, and liberalization of foreign direct investment. On the American side, the principal emphasis has been on policies affecting savings and investment, with major stress on the role of the chronic federal deficits in reducing national savings, and on improving primary and secondary education to improve the American labor force.

All these initiatives — multilateral (GATT), regional (EC), and bilateral (U.S. and Japan) — represent efforts to achieve a more integrated global economy. The need for such adaptation is so compelling that unilateral measures are also being taken. But unilateral actions are likely to run into political resistance if they exacerbate inequities between firms in different countries. Here, too, multilateral agreements which furnish benefits to all participants offer the greatest hope for success.

Recent examples like the B.C.C.I. scandal reveal the incentives to move operations to the countries with the loosest regulatory standards, and the havoc these difference can wreak on the international economy. That issue was sharpened during Congressional debates over the Administration's request for "fast track" authority to negotiate a United States-Mexico Free Trade Agreement when many asked: How can Mexico be granted unimpeded access to the U.S. market when producers in Mexico do not face the costs incurred by American producers in complying with stricter domestic environmental and occupational health and safety standards? The Administration's response in the context of the free-trade negotiations has been to seek to raise the standards of Mexico rather than lower our own.

Advantages that foreign firms have because of looser regulations should be removed to the greatest extent possible. But which ones? And how? The classic case for trade in accordance with the principle of comparative advantage is based on the differences between nations. Although the main differences are in resource endowments, including the knowledge and skills of the population, divergent institutional environments also affect comparative advantage. Efforts to equalize these regulations can in some instances reduce excessive government regulation or taxation, but in other cases, such as environmental standards or prudential supervision of banking, they can induce a risky lowering of standards.

When these dissimilarities genuinely stem from the special social preferences of individual countries and will not excessively harm third parties, they should be seen as legitimate determinants of comparative advantage. However, great efforts should be made to prevent countries from pursuing protectionist policies under this guise of social preference. For example, in recent months, the EC has attempted to establish many uniform social policies for the entire Community, such as minimum wages, Sunday closing laws, minimum pensions, minimum vacations, and standard sales taxes. These policies may reflect genuine social preferences, but they are a particularly onerous burden to place on competing countries, particularly less developed ones, that cannot afford them.

The challenge for the post Uruguay Round global economy is to determine how to deal with these international competitive advantages arising from differences in national regulations and structures. The solution must try to respect the social preferences of individual nations and provide adequate standards to protect the health and welfare of people everywhere, without placing some countries at a competitive disadvantage.

The idea of selective harmonization underlies the EC approach to creating a single market. In some fields, the principle of mutual recognition of existing national standards is being established; while in others, harmonization is the goal. A combination of the two principles is a third option. In the financial services sector, for example, the Community has attempted to harmonize essential standards of authorization, supervision, and prudential rules to safeguard shareholders or depositors, but to provide for mutual recognition of home-country control on the basis of those rules.

More generally, three steps are needed to adequately confront the issue. The first is to determine what types of government measures to address. Given that virtually every government policy can be shown to have *some* effect on trade and investment, it is essential to limit post Uruguay Round negotiations to those measures that *substantially* affect international competition and the health and welfare of the world's citizens, such as blatant subsidies, certain anti-trust policies, product safety standards, environmental standards, financial regulations, and investment rules.

The second step is to determine what policies should be adopted when significant national differences exist. If harmonization is to be sought, at what level — the lowest level of regulation, the highest, or somewhere in between? In which cases should one follow the European Community's approach of mutual recognition — as in professional certification — provided that certain minimum standards are met?

The third step is to determine what is the correct international forum for pursuing this program. Given the size and diversity of its membership and its special mission for free trade, GATT is the logical forum but may be too unwieldy a body for negotiations on highly sensitive domestic policies.[4] The OECD, in linking economies at a more comparable stage of development, may be preferable, although negotiations on domestic policies should be open not only to its own members but to all countries prepared to accept the goal of modifying domestic policies to advance international trade and investment even if a transition period is required. The OECD would have to broaden its outreach to accommodate this enlarged role.

The United States should not give up on GATT, however. If the right kind of improvements can be effected in the GATT mechanism, it might be able to achieve more of what needs to be done. For example, a GATT with a broader range of responsibilities covering not

---

NATIONAL LAW VS. INTERNATIONAL AGREEMENT

The conflict between national policy and global economic integration is demonstrated by a recent case involving U.S. protection of marine mammals. In 1991, the United States restricted tuna imports of predominantly Mexican tuna-fishing companies through U.S. implementation of the Marine Mammals Protection Act (MMPA). The ensuing problems illustrate the type of disputes that will arise more often as nations sweep away formal barriers to trade (such as tariffs). Differing national policies — regarding the environment, financial regulation, and a host of other issues — will increasingly become the chief impediments to international flows of goods and services.

The MMPA, which was enacted in 1972, contains amendments designed to curtail the accidental killing of dolphins and other marine mammals caught in commercial fishing nets. It prohibits imports from any tuna company in the East Tropical Pacific fleet that exceeds stringent U.S. standards on dolphin killings by tuna-fishing ships. The MMPA also forbids tuna imports from intermediaries — countries that import tuna caught in violation of the law and then export it to the United States. The U.S. Government, which initially refused to implement the Act, was sued by the Earth Island Institute, a California-based lobbying group. The precedent set by an early victory, and a string of other judgments, forced the administration to adhere to the MMPA. Greatly increased barriers to tuna imports resulted.

Because this U.S. law may have violated GATT rules, Mexico has taken the United States to the GATT dispute resolution panel. GATT's Article XX recognizes that environmental objectives can be a legitimate reasons for restricting trade, but the panel indicates that it may rule in favor of Mexico. As a result, bilateral negotiations between the United States and Mexico have attempted to reopen tuna trade and develop more stringent tuna-fishing standards for Mexico.

One of the primary challenges to further integration of the global economy will be reconciling the goal of greater growth and commerce with differing national and international objectives. Although sovereign nations should most definitely retain the right to identify national priorities, such laws and regulations should not become a back door to protectionism. It is also critical that future international agreements on new priorities seek some harmony with international economic agreements such as GATT. Currently, this is not the case; only 17 of the 127 major international environmental agreements take open trade provisions into account.[5]

only trade in goods and services but also aspects of international investment, would offer a broader scope for trade-offs and a fuller basket of mutual benefits to consider. Over time, that should lead to more constructive agreements. Therefore, **we encourage the U.S. government and its negotiators to press for a broader GATT, which should over time become the institutional framework for a new world trade and investment organization.**

ENVIRONMENTAL STANDARDS AND TRADE

As protection of the global environment has moved higher on many national agendas, the developed countries of North America and Europe have taken some profound measures to reduce the output of pollutants, sometimes as the result of international agreements, sometimes exclusively as domestic policy initiatives. In the United States, the Clean Air Act of 1963 and its 1970 revisions have played a significant role in bringing down emissions of major pollutants. Individual states have environmental laws that go even further than the federal standards. Improved standards carry a benefit to U.S. citizens; but these improvements have been very costly, and some fear that the environmental premium contained in some American products has put them at a disadvantage to goods produced in countries with lower environmental standards.

In an earlier policy statement, CED has supported the general principles adopted by the OECD for such concerns among the industrialized countries. This approach concedes that differential environmental standards are legitimate reflections of the diverse levels of income among countries and that barriers to trade such as countervailing duties are not appropriate. **We recognize that different pollution standards can be an advantage or disadvantage in international trade. Nevertheless, we support the principle that pollution-abatement costs should be included in prices to more fully reflect the social costs of production.**[6]

The fear of an unfair trade advantage because of excessively tolerant environmental standards was expressed in the United States in relation to Mexican participation in NAFTA. Critics have observed that Mexico's softer regulations and lax enforcement create cost differentials which will lure factories and jobs south of the border. Seeking to allay these concerns, the Mexican government has stressed that it is increasing the financial resources available for enforcement and is generally prosecuting its responsibilities more aggressively in this area. The Administration also moved to reassure critics of NAFTA by giving environmental concerns a high priority in the negotiations.[7] These reassurances helped the Administration to secure extension of fast-track negotiating procedures from Congress.

A number of other less advanced countries in Latin America and Eastern Europe have expressed an interest negotiating free trade agreements with the United States. Freer access to the U.S. and other advanced countries' markets offers advantages to these countries in higher growth and living standards for their citizens. However, fears continue that looser environmental standards may reduce sales and production in more advanced countries with higher standards and force them to produce other goods. Because of the potential damage that these standards could inflict on the world's environment, this appears to be an area for mutually advantageous accommodation, in which *increased* market access is provided in exchange for higher environmental standards. In the longer term, it may be less costly to industrialize while adhering to environmental standards than to reduce pollution after industrialization. Both developed and less developed countries might then enjoy the benefits of freer trade and less pollution, leaving a more prosperous and safer world for future generations.

AN EMERGING REGIONALISM

Although the United States has been a leading proponent of strengthening GATT as an instrument to reduce barriers to international trade and investment, U.S. negotiators have recently begun to pursue regional trading initiatives, specifically, a North American Free Trade Agreement including Mexico and Canada and the nascent Enterprise for the

Americas initiative. This U.S. focus on regional economic arrangements, the European Community's progress toward achieving a single regional market, and Japan's increasing investment in Asia have fostered fears that the three major economic powers will devote increased energy to developing integrated regional trading arrangements, at the expense of GATT.

CED has long supported freer trade with Mexico, provided that any agreement serves to lift Mexico's environment and work-safety standards and acknowledges the different levels of development in each country. Such an agreement would offer substantial political benefits to the United States, in addition to an economic boost. Mexico's long border with the United States makes its economic development and political stability an important step in addressing environmental problems, illegal immigration, and drug trafficking.[8]

Although regional arrangements could be a tool for liberalizing trade, the United States should continue to place the highest priority on economic integration through multilateral instruments. As the world's largest exporter, the United States has global concerns; and due to the size of its market, America can exert unmatched influence on the negotiation of broader global agreements. For two distinct reasons, regional agreements are less than optimal.

Regional arrangements do not reflect the realities of today's U.S. or world economy. Because of advances in technology, telecommunications, and transportation, international economic activity no longer follows simple geographic patterns. Much of the growth of world trade over the past ten years has occurred between the so-called "blocs" rather than between member nations of the same bloc.[9] However, if regional blocs complement the global system and increase trade, they can spur the global system to liberalize world trading rules.

Furthermore, the international economic powers are too reliant on global markets to focus exclusively on regional trade. Although the United States has significant political motivation to include Mexico in

NAFTA, the longer-term economic benefits could also be substantial. Similarly, although Japan has invested heavily in other Pacific Rim countries, its primary interest is in maintaining access to markets throughout the world.*

*Regional trading arrangements that are trade diverting threaten to aggravate the poverty of less developed nations excluded from all three regions.*** Although participants in the blocs would see marginal gains or losses, depending on the structure of the agreements, nations excluded from the system would suffer severe consequences.[10] Because it seeks to include developing nations, the Enterprise for the Americas initiative could answer some of these concerns, but it still leaves open the status of developing countries outside the Western Hemisphere. The United States has assumed a much more progressive stance than the Western Europeans who have balked at including the Eastern European countries in their union and ignored the sub-Saharan countries.

A system of preferential regional trading blocs that failed to include on an equal basis the less-developed nations of sub-Saharan Africa and South Asia or the emerging market economies of Eastern Europe would deprive these nations of equal access to the world's most lucrative markets and would impede efforts to relieve their poverty. Moreover, it would be ironic for the industrial nations that have long trumpeted the value of free markets to exclude countries that have recently accepted our economic vision. Conversely, regional agreements could also diminish incentives for U.S. exporters to seek out markets in the developing world, where much of the world's population growth is expected to take place in the next thirty years.

Accordingly, any U.S. attempts to craft additional free trade agreements (FTAs) should be governed by four principles. First, to the maximum extent possible, they should be trade-creating rather than trade-diverting. Simply replacing competitive foreign products from one country with more-favored products from another will not benefit American consumers. Second, any regional arrangement

---

*See memorandum by RODERICK M. HILLS, (page 88).

**See memorandum by WALTER Y. ELISHA, (page 88).

should be a complement, not an alternative, to global and multilateral agreements such as GATT. Third, no regional arrangement should be allowed to become a vehicle for protectionist barriers. Fourth, these regional agreements need not be confined to the countries in closest physical proximity to the United States: there is no economic rationale for freer trade with Chile than with Korea. **Both to act as a rallier of nations and to serve its own interests, the United States should be ready to mutually reduce trade barriers through agreements with countries both inside and outside of our hemisphere.***

While these goals are laudable, their implementation is complicated by political realities. Our recent experiences in gaining domestic support for a Free Trade Agreement with Mexico, and in negotiating an FTA with Canada, have demonstrated that regional arrangements can be exceedingly difficult to negotiate. For example, as the final stages of the NAFTA negotiations were evolving, there was reason to be concerned about certain features being incorporated into the agreement. Inherent in any free trade area is preferential treatment for its members whose products are not subject to tariffs applying against outsiders. In order to determine which products qualify for free trade among the members, "rules of origin" (i.e., domestic content standards) are required. However, in a number of sectors the rules of origin being adopted are so stringent that they may constitute a steeper barrier to imports from non-members than existed before.

Clearly, the primary U.S. focus should remain on improving the global trading system, but U.S. policy makers should continue to pursue sub-GATT agreements. If the Uruguay Round fails, these agreements can serve both as a means to increase the efficiency of the world economy and as an example of the benefits of freer trade that might motivate a better multilateral agreement. In short, *good* regional arrangements could help the global trading system achieve consensus on the benefits of freer trade.

Because the United States helped build the global trading system, other nations are espe-

cially sensitive to our policy initiatives. If we fail to demonstrate leadership in maintaining an open global system, we encourage other nations to focus their attention on developing inward-looking regional alternatives to the detriment of the world economy.

AN INTERNATIONAL INVESTMENT ACCORD

Foreign trade and direct investment are inextricably linked. Both are means of making the best use of national resources. Moreover, the huge increase in the number of multinational corporations has bound the world economy more closely together; about half of world exports of nonagricultural products originates in companies that are units of multinational enterprises and about a quarter consists of transactions *between* units of individual multinationals. Most major companies take it as routine that foreign markets can be served through either exports or sales from foreign affiliates. In the case of U.S. firms, sales from their affiliates in Europe exceed their exports to Europe from the United States by a factor of more than seven to one.

Through much of the post World War II period, the United States was the dominant country of origin for foreign direct investment. In recent years, however, there have been large increases in foreign direct investment in the United States. As a result, the United States is today both the largest home country for originating foreign direct investment and the largest host country.

International investment has taken on added importance recently as a result of the growth of regional economic arrangements, such as customs unions and free-trade zones, that inherently discriminate against the trade of nonmember countries. Foreign direct investment can overcome this discrimination by establishing subsidiaries within one or more of the member countries to serve the entire regional market. Much recent U.S. and Japanese investment in the EC has been driven by the desire to avoid discriminatory barriers.

Despite the close links between trade and investment, there is no set of multilateral rules governing international investment compa-

*See memorandum by RODERICK M. HILLS, (page 89).

rable to the GATT rules for international trade. Instead, the United States is party to a number of bilateral investment treaties as well as a "soft law" arrangement in the form of nonmandatory guidelines for the multinational enterprises of the advanced industrial countries.

Although there has been a trend toward liberalization of government policies on foreign direct investment, nationalistic opposition to foreign investment is far from dead.[11] In both the United States and Europe, pressures exist to restrict Japanese and other foreign investment by imposing discriminatory requirements for their establishment and operation. Both the United States and European countries contend that the Japanese discriminate against direct investment in Japan. In developing countries, the traditional policy of confrontation with foreign ("colonial") investors has largely given way to a more pragmatic approach, but the legacy of an anticolonialist tradition still creates problems. The temptations for governments, businesses, and labor unions to play on nationalistic emotions are strong everywhere.

For these reasons, **preparatory steps should be taken now to negotiate a comprehensive international investment accord among all the OECD nations to constrain nationalistic desires to limit foreign direct investment.** Like-minded countries outside the OECD could participate in the negotiations or be associated with such an accord when they felt ready to abide by its rules. The new investment regime could be part of a broader effort to deal with domestic policies that impede international trade and investment.

DIRECTIONS FOR POLICY*

1. Research and experience have demonstrated that open markets are the best means of ensuring economic growth, prosperity, and peace. The long-term aim of American trade policy should be the integration of the world economy. Protectionism, under whatever label, would frustrate that aim at a heavy cost to all nations. In contrast with those who argue that this country can no longer afford open markets and should adopt more interventionist domestic and trade policies, CED believes such policies would run counter to the market principles on which the U.S. economy is based and would fall prey to pork-barrel politics. Ultimately, such policies would impede rather than enhance our economic ·vitality. However, the United States must react swiftly and effectively to nations that restrict access to their markets.

2. The removal of unfair trading practices is vital to U.S. competitiveness. Unfair trade takes the form of restrictions on market access, dumping, subsidies, and infringement of intellectual property rights. These practices may inflict severe damage or ruin on otherwise competitive domestic industries in another country. Rather than imitating such predatory practices or engaging in industrial policy or managed trade, the United States should use the GATT remedial process to the maximum extent possible. Where that option is unavailable or too slow and cumbersome, we should be prepared to aggressively use our statutes to open markets abroad (Section 301), to discourage unfair penetration of our domestic market through dumping and subsidization, and to deter the infringement of U.S. intellectual property rights. However, we should limit the definition of dumping to selling in foreign markets at lower prices than at home and should not resort to the unfair trade laws as instruments of outright protection.

3. To promote global integration, multilateral trade agreements are the best approach. Bilateral and regional free-trade arrangements, may serve as building blocks for an integrated global trading system if they avoid raising barriers against outsiders and otherwise conform to GATT requirements. Moreover unless there are compelling political reasons, as in Mexico's case, these sub-GATT agreements should not be offered only to our closest geographical neighbors, but rather to any country meeting the necessary economic criteria that is willing to negotiate a fair agreement. The highest immediate priority of U.S. trade policy, however, is the successful completion of the

---

*See memorandum by WILLIAM D. EBERLE, (page 89).

Uruguay Round of multilateral trade negotiations. If the Uruguay Round opens the way for freer trade in agricultural products, textiles and clothing, services, and intellectual property, it will foster the international trade and economic growth of both the technologically advanced and the developing countries, reinvigorate the world economy, and greatly reduce pressures for discriminatory trading arrangements.

4. As a further step toward integrating the global economy, corporations based in different home countries should be free to establish themselves in foreign countries under conditions and rules that apply equally to domestic companies. The United States should lead an effort to harmonize the regulatory and structural burdens that companies face across the globe. However, it is important that there not be a downward spiral toward the lowest level of regulation, leaving the health and welfare of people everywhere at risk. This is especially true in industries, such as banking, where the stability of the system is involved.

5. There is no world organization for foreign investment that promotes liberalization, has a common set of rules, and provides a judicial body for resolving disputes between nations as GATT for trade. We therefore recommend that preparatory steps now be taken in the OECD to negotiate a comprehensive international investment accord. There is urgent need for such an accord to combat nationalistic opposition to foreign investment in many countries and to enable businesses to compete globally through both trade and investment. The negotiation of the accord should be open to all countries that share the objective of an open global investment regime.

B. MACROECONOMIC POLICY AND EXCHANGE RATES

Virtually all nations of the world pursue the goal of economic growth. Growth—and growth alone—creates the additional resources that make it possible for the United States and the rest of the world to accomplish what we regard as fundamental goals: higher living standards, individual national security, greater national and international social equity, a cleaner environment, and more liberal and open economies and societies. But the growth of individual economies, including that of the United States, is increasingly driven by the global expansion that provides domestic producers with larger markets and wider access to capital, technology, and labor.

The United States and its partners therefore have an obligation to pursue macroeconomic policies, including an exchange rate system, aimed at keeping the world economy moving forward at a healthy pace with a freer flow of trade and investment. We favor two strategies to strengthen and maintain global economic growth. First, in most countries, but especially the United States, efforts should be made to increase national saving and thereby productive investment. Second, in today's integrated, interdependent world, the policy actions of several nations taken independently may be incompatible not only in terms of global economic performance but also in terms of their own domestic goals. Deepening integration of the global economy demands better international cooperation in designing and implementing macroeconomic policies.

A WORLD-WIDE CAPITAL SHORTAGE

A higher rate of capital formation in the industrial countries will serve not only their own interests but also, through the global growth mechanism of expanded markets, the interests of the developing countries, the newly industrialized countries of Asia, and the new states of Eastern Europe and the former Soviet Union, which are striving to modernize and establish closer links with the world economy. And higher rates of capital formation in the developing and newly market-oriented economies are critical to their economic success and, in many cases, to their political viability.

In seeking to promote world growth and integration, economic policy makers face the major obstacle of a worldwide capital shortage. This shortage stems from a number of interrelated factors: declining rates of personal saving throughout the industrial countries, large national budget deficits (a form of dissaving) that deplete the resources available for real investment in productive resources,[12] growing demands for capital to help unite Germany and to rebuild Eastern Europe and the former Soviet Union, and rising demands for capital throughout the industrial world to replace obsolete plant and equipment and to improve the physical and social infrastructure of highways, airports, bridges, power systems, communications networks, sewers and waste disposal plants, schools, hospitals, and much else. The combination of a slowly growing supply and rapidly increasing demand for capital is reflected in high long-term real interest rates.

Over the longer term, increasing life expectancy in the industrial countries will contribute to strains by reducing the size of the working population relative to the number of retired workers. This trend will increase consumption and require the substitution of capital for labor. The capital shortage may also be aggravated by weaknesses in the world banking system; as banks seek to improve their capital ratios, their ability to lend will be squeezed.*

Overcoming the world capital shortage will require most industrial nations to adopt measures for increasing rates of saving, reducing and finally eliminating their budget deficits, and cutting unproductive public expenditures and wasteful uses of national resources. Above all, it will require growth.

INCREASING U.S. SAVING AND CAPITAL FORMATION

The United States, still the largest and most important economy in the world, needs to play a constructive role in raising global saving and

---

*See memorandum by FRANKLIN A. LINDSAY, (page 89).

capital formation. In the 1980s America's net national saving rate collapsed, falling from about 8 percent of national income in the 1950-1979 period to about 3 percent in 1990 because of both large federal budget deficits and lower private saving. Proportionally, the United States saves far less as a nation than any of the other major industrial countries; in the 1980s our net saving rate averaged about one-fifth that of Japan, and about one-third that of Germany and the Group of Seven (G-7) nations (Figure 6).

Low saving and investment rates have weakened American economic performance. When a nation does not save enough to finance its domestic investment, the difference must be made up by borrowing from abroad. The greater its internal budget deficit and the lower its private saving rate relative to private investment, the greater its dependence on foreign saving. The United States, once the largest source of capital to other countries, has become the world's largest debtor. Instead of exporting capital to the developing world, with

great reciprocal benefits for our own exporting industries, we now absorb capital from abroad, putting great upward pressure on long-term interest rates and slowing worldwide investment.

America's external deficits could not have grown so large nor endured so long had it not been for foreigners' willingness to invest in dollar assets. This reflected the international role of the dollar and relative confidence in America's political stability and long-run growth potential. We must move decisively to justify that confidence — or risk seeing it shattered, with ruinous results. Our top priority for the rest of this decade should be eliminating the budget deficits that have undermined our saving rates, our long-term investment, and world economic growth. Unless remedied, our chronic budget deficits and low national saving rate will act as a drag on our productivity growth and our ability to build any international cohesion on critical economic issues.

Therefore, U.S. economic policy should ultimately aim at raising the rate of national

Figure 6

Net National Saving
1962-90

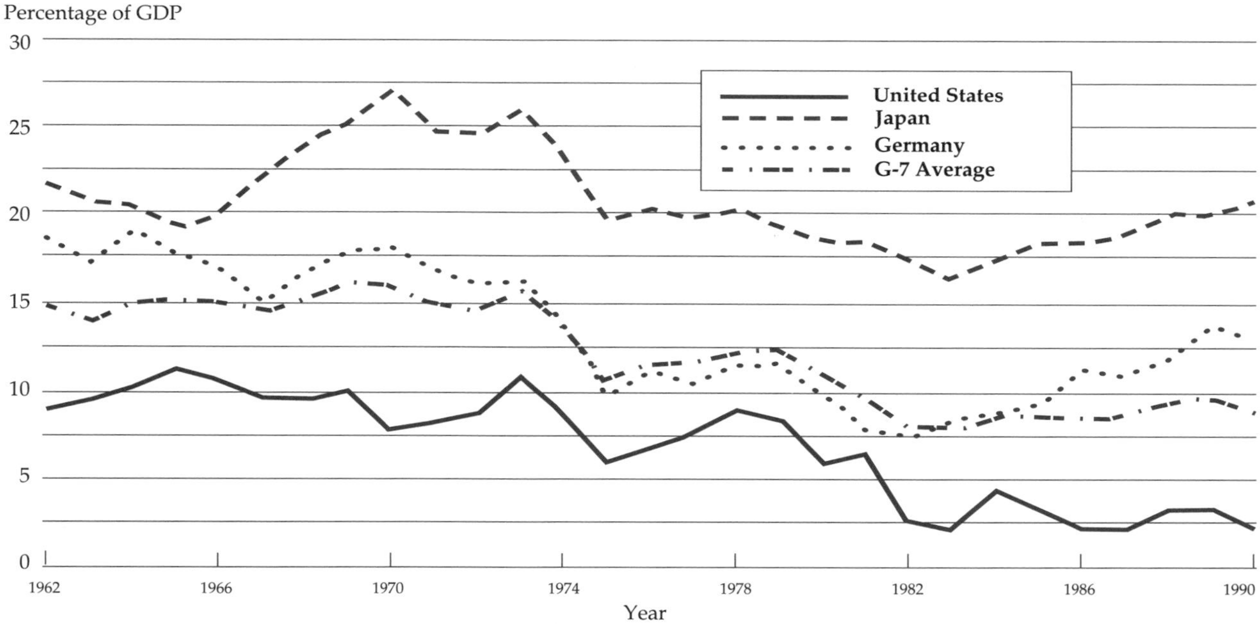

Percentage of GDP

SOURCE: OECD National Accounts

saving at least to its pre-1980 average of about 8 percent of national income, about 5 percentage points above its current level.

The additional saving, when productively invested, would raise the annual growth rates of productivity and GDP by 0.5 to 1 percent. That may sound modest, but such an improvement would raise the long-term growth rate by 25 to 50 percent. This would make possible a steady increase in living standards, a steady reduction of unemployment, and extra capital for meeting our domestic and foreign needs. Indeed, this is an ambitious saving target relative to our recent behavior; it will require movement toward federal budgetary surplus and perhaps an increase in private saving as well.[13]

The top priority in raising national saving must be first to reduce and finally to eliminate the structural budget deficit, the deficit that would remain even if the economy were operating at full capacity and full employment. Figure 7 highlights the large increases in the structural deficit during the 1980s. Our aim

should be to achieve a budget surplus, including the Social Security and other retirement accounts, of 1 to 2 percent of GDP within a decade. Elimination of the budget deficit is the surest way to increase national saving and capital formation.

We believe that these national and federal saving targets should be met to the greatest extent possible through spending reductions rather than tax increases. Domestic spending should be reduced except in programs that contribute to productive investment and economic growth or have a compelling public purpose. We recognize — and stress elsewhere in this statement — that some urgent domestic needs, like human resource development, will require more public resources, not less. But we believe that these needs can be met principally by transferring resources from lower-priority programs.

Similarly, military spending should be reduced as much as possible consistent with the less threatening post cold war national security environment. This peace dividend should

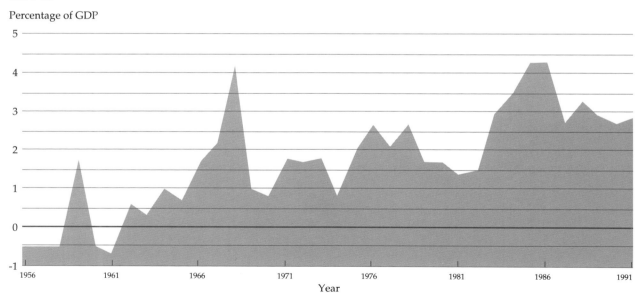

Figure 7

The Structural Federal Budget Deficit
1950-91

Percentage of GDP

SOURCE: U.S. Office of Management and Budget, 1947-61;
Congressional Budget Office, 1962-91

37

be used for deficit reduction, thereby raising national saving and investment.[14] Military expenditures must be continually reviewed in light of changing national security requirements and competing private and public investment requirements. **The United States cannot afford to spend more on defense than is absolutely required for genuine national security purposes.** In particular, the defense budget must not become a jobs program with spending levels rationalized by misapplied economic arguments. It will be a tragically wasted opportunity if we fail to transfer resources desperately needed for investment and growth out of military uses because of opposition to economic adjustment. This would not only waste resources but also create pressures for otherwise unnecessary tax

increases. Existing assistance programs should be used, and augmented if necessary, to facilitate this adjustment;[15] such assistance will be temporary and much less costly than unnecessary military spending. Also, if the assistance aims to improve the quality of America's human capital by retraining those affected by cutbacks, it will benefit the economy as a whole.

Finally, although CED believes that deficit reduction must first and foremost emphasize spending cuts, we continue to hold that "carefully designed tax increases that do not discourage private saving and investment will do less harm to the economy than persistent structural budget deficits, provided we have political discipline sufficient to prevent those increased revenues from being spent."[16] **If aggressive pursuit of domestic and military**

DISLOCATED WORKERS

Although both the integration of the global economy and the cuts in defense spending made possible by the end of the Cold War will benefit our economy in the long run, some American workers and communities will suffer. The price of adapting our economy to a changed world will be paid in jobs lost by workers in uncompetitive or obsolete businesses. Because the businesses themselves often lack either the resources or the incentives to get these workers back on their feet, the federal government needs to take the lead in enabling displaced workers to contribute to the economy. This can best be accomplished by stepping up efforts to invest in displaced workers, not by raising barriers to trade or continuing to build weapons systems that we do not need. Our goal must be to help people respond to a changing economy, not to avoid it.

The main federal response to these shifts has been the *Economic Dislocation and Worker Adjustment Act*, a comprehensive array of retraining and re-employment services derived from Title III of the Job Training Partnership Act. Enacted in 1988, the EDWAA helps dislocated workers who are unlikely to return to their previous industries or occupations. Originally conceived to help the approximately 1.8 million workers each year who lose their jobs due to plant closings or relocations, elimination of a position or shift, or slack work, Congress ex-

tended the program in 1991 to cover displaced defense workers.

The EDWAA seeks to help dislocated workers by providing a range of services aimed at getting the worker back into the work force. These programs include: boosting worker skills through both job-specific retraining programs and basic education and enabling workers to find new jobs through a variety of reemployment services.

By emphasizing skill development and allowing for local flexibility, the EDWAA provides a valuable framework for government assistance to dislocated workers. However, the program is vastly underfunded, serving only 9% of eligible workers. Unfortunately, many of these workers use only the reemployment services, since income support during full time training is often not available.[17]

Although it is too soon to gauge its effectiveness, EDWAA serves as an important framework for treatment of displaced workers. If EDWAA is to meet the demands of all American workers hurt by shifts in international trade or cuts in defense, the program needs to be adequately funded. Since a broader skill base will be a critical condition for higher future wages, it must also encourage dislocated workers to seek additional training.[18]

spending reductions is insufficient to reduce the deficit substantially, national saving should be raised by tax increases.

IS A HIGHER-SAVING U.S. ECONOMY VIABLE?

As federal expenditure or tax programs that sustain public and private consumption are reduced, the nation's output must be shifted from consumption to investments in both physical and human capital. Can policies to reduce consumption and increase saving and investment be successful, especially if the economy is suffering from unemployment? If public and private consumption spending, including military spending, is reduced, will investment spending rise to replace it? Or would we face inadequate total demand, resulting in a loss of production and jobs?

This problem of underconsumption received considerable attention during the Great Depression and afterward, and we hear echoes of it today from those who claim that low-priority military or domestic spending cannot be cut because of the loss of jobs and income. However, this argument misrepresents the situation. Underconsumption is not our problem. Indeed, private consumption expenditures now take a higher proportion of our national income than at any time in the past half century. Our policy objective should be to *shift* some of our economic resources from consumption to investment for growth, because, in the long run, such productive investments lead to greater job creation than consumption does. Without such investment, national income will not continue to increase. Since Americans have grown accustomed to increasing national prosperity — and increased consumption — there would be more demands on a limited pie, rather than the continually growing pie that investment can bring.

We recognize that the transition to a high-investment, high-growth economy must be gradual and may require programs to assist adjustment. However, we categorically reject the notion that lower-priority public or private consumption spending is required for economic prosperity. First, some of the increased investment, such as that in infrastructure, education, and training, will be undertaken publicly, although often more appropriately at the state and local levels than the federal level. Second, postwar experience in the United States and other countries shows that a properly designed mix of macroeconomic policies, with more fiscal restraint and less monetary stringency, can maintain aggregate demand through stronger private investment and exports.[19]

The long-term problem made acute by economic globalization is not so much maintaining aggregate demand as raising domestic investment in activities that generate strong productivity growth and high-paying jobs. Increasing savings per se may not automatically raise the level of domestic investment commensurately, although it will stimulate investment through lower interest rates. In the integrated global economy, capital saved in the United States can readily be invested abroad. In short, domestic investment must be *earned* in global competition. Thus higher national saving will raise *American* productivity and wages *only* if the United States provides attractive investment opportunities for our saving and that of other countries. This means that higher national saving, by itself, is not enough. Investments in human capital, technology, and public infrastructure must be made which will make capital highly productive in the United States. (For a more detailed discussion, see Chapter 4.)

INTERNATIONAL COOPERATION IN MACROECONOMIC POLICY

Every Western government has accepted, formally or de facto, the responsibility of employing macroeconomic policies to combat inflation and unemployment. International cooperation has helped to overcome political opportunism, the pressures of interest groups, and the inherent unpredictability of capitalist economic systems to help make the postwar stabilization and growth performance of the industrial nations much better than before World War II.

The problem of policy making for stable economic growth has now expanded from the national to the global level. Major national governments and central banks can be expected to continue to strive for policies aimed at domestic noninflationary growth; but in an interdependent world, they increasingly must also work together to achieve those ends.

As we noted in Chapter 2, the interdependence resulting from economic integration has greatly reduced the effective autonomy of even large national economies, including that of the United States. Nations have found that their policies now are less potent domestically, affect other countries more strongly, and produce sharp and often unwelcome changes in the trade and payments balances and exchange rates which link them with others.

Interdependence thus means that each country has lost significant control over its own economic destiny and, in turn, finds its economy affected by the actions of others, over which it has no direct control. Twenty-five years ago, "when America sneezed the rest of the world caught pneumonia;" and only other countries had to worry about "the gnomes of Zurich," a caricature of foreign owners or managers of capital. Today, the United States has no immunity from economic ills abroad, and the "gnomes" allocating the world's capital have branched out from New York, London, and Zurich to Tokyo, Hong Kong, Singapore, and dozens of other financial and business centers around the globe.

In this changed world, cooperation among the major economies in policy making has become increasingly important. However, cooperation can take a variety of forms, ranging from sharing information to the coordination of policies through joint decision making. Information sharing allows each country to take account of the likely policies of others and thereby improve its own (and presumably aggregate) decisions. However, at least in principle, a stronger form of cooperation through joint decisions on national fiscal, monetary, and exchange rate policies could further improve overall economic performance with respect to growth, inflation, and payments imbalances. Successful policy coordination, in theory, would leave every country better off than if each acted independently, a result not of altruism but of cooperative self-interest.[20]

In spite of the apparent theoretical advantages of macroeconomic policy coordination, its use has been generally limited to coordinated exchange rate intervention rather than joint decisions on fiscal and monetary policies, and its effectiveness is in dispute.[21] Its limited application may, in some part, be due to a failure of policy makers to think in terms required by an integrated global economy and to recognize the erosion of national economic autonomy. However, there are more immediate limitations. First, widespread international economic difficulties are not necessarily due to an "international problem." For instance, although 1991 and 1992 may have been the weakest years for international growth in decades, the pervasive economic weakness appears related more to special and different problems in the United States, Japan and Germany. In such cases, it is difficult to identify and organize a cooperative solution, although there may be scope for one in principle. As the ineffective nature of the G-7 summits in recent years demonstrates, it is difficult to achieve effective policy coordination among major countries when domestic economic policy corrections that face strong opposition at home are required. Differences in perception of economic conditions and mechanisms, in national goals, in the distribution of gains and costs from coordination constitute serious obstacles to successful coordination.[22] For instance, the inflexibility of fiscal policy in the United States has proven a major stumbling block to reducing our large trade imbalances, and the unresponsiveness of Japanese imports to conventional policy measures has impeded adjustment.

Even among the European countries who are looking toward monetary union in accordance with the Maastricht Treaty, the coordination of macroeconomic policy is proving to be exceedingly difficult. Germany's high interest rates at a time of widespread European economic sluggishness reflects its determination to fight inflation rather than stimulate broader economic recovery.

EXCHANGE RATE STABILITY

The problems of interdependence have been most evident with respect to exchange rate policies. To hold together a global economy in which nations have the power to pursue their own fiscal and monetary policies and experience widely varying rates of inflation and growth, the world needs an exchange rate system flexible enough to prevent gross misalignments but stable enough to permit trade and investment to flow freely in an interdependent world. How to create an exchange rate system that will be both flexible and stable is an extremely difficult and complex problem.

After the breakdown of the Bretton Woods system in the early 1970s, many economists contended that floating exchange rates would obviate the need for close economic cooperation among nations. The abandonment of fixed rates would supposedly free each of the major industrial countries to pursue its own domestic goals for growth, employment, and price stability. The reasoning was that floating rates would allow countries to pursue independent monetary and fiscal policies while the adjustment of payments imbalances would be achieved through movements in exchange rates.

This view was oriented to an older world in which trade in goods and services and relatively stable long-term capital movements dominated external transactions. The global integration of capital and money markets has created a new world, however, in which exchange rates are driven in large part by enormous capital transactions, not all of which reflect "fundamental" factors such as national differences in saving and trade and investment balances. In practice, with such a vast amount of exchange rate activity being carried on by traders at major banks and multinational corporations, whether for speculative or for risk-management reasons, short-term foreign exchange rate movements appear to have lost much of their relationship to the underlying factors that ultimately govern the current and long-term capital accounts.

Experience has shown that in this new world, freely floating exchange rates do not necessarily produce external balance or reduce economic interdependence. Figure 8 suggests that the market exchange rate can deviate for extended periods from what is presumably a more stable and fundamental relationship.

Figure 8

Value of the Dollar:
Purchasing Power Parity Index vs. Market Exchange Rate

U.S. vs. Germany, in DM per U.S. Dollar

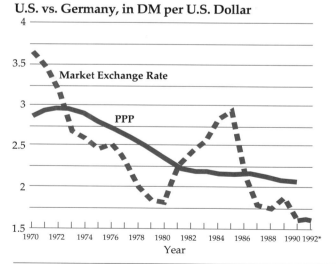

U.S. vs. Japan, in Yen per U.S. Dollar

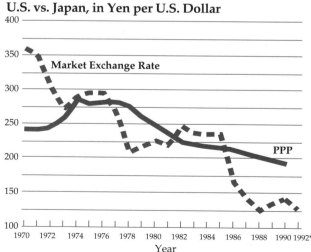

*1992 market exchange rates are averages of the January-June monthly averages

SOURCE: 1970-91: OECD; 1992: Federal Reserve

41

In the early 1980s, when the United States pursued expansionary fiscal policy and a policy of benign neglect toward exchange rates, the dollar rapidly appreciated, causing severe dislocations in the domestic and global economies. The domestic dislocations spurred calls for protectionism that threatened the future of open trade, and structural imbalances resulted. Dissatisfaction with this situation led to the Plaza Agreement of 1985, in which the United States, Japan, West Germany, Britain, and France expressed their intention to intervene jointly on the foreign exchange market to bring about a depreciation of the dollar. This was followed by a mixed system within the G-7 of partially managed rates with informal agreements on unannounced exchange rate targets accompanied by consultation on macroeconomic policies. It has become apparent that interdependence requires some degree of mutual accommodation and coordination. Money does not manage itself globally anymore than it does nationally and regionally.

The advantages of exchange rate stability have been shown by the European Community. In 1979, the EC established the European Monetary System (EMS). The primary operational aim of the EMS was to constrain the movements of exchange rates within a relatively narrow band except in the most extreme cases. The EMS was not designed to produce exchange rates that would *correct* extreme economic imbalances (only major exchange rate realignments can help in that extremity); rather, it was intended to help *prevent* such major imbalances by treating small exchange rate movements as signalling the need for corrective fiscal and monetary actions.

Despite much skepticism before the system began to function, the EMS has worked well, particularly in recent years when the bands have held steady. Holding exchange rates within the bands has effectively meant that European monetary policies have followed the leadership of the Bundesbank. One major result has been comparatively low inflation in the continental European countries and a general strengthening of their currencies relative to the dollar. Another has been the steady progress toward economic integration. Long

before EMS, the new United States of America, of course, demonstrated the critical importance to economic integration and growth of a unified monetary system.

However, the advantages of exchange rate stability, do not guarantee the success of international efforts to create or maintain a regime of stable rates. The lesson of recent history is that no exchange rate system, fixed or floating, can function well if highly inappropriate national macroeconomic policies are followed. Just as the 1980s revealed problems with floating rates, the earlier collapse of the Bretton Woods system demonstrated that a regime with relatively fixed rates does not guarantee the adjustment of national policies or the timely adjustment of rates and may not be viable without such adjustment. Further floating exchange rates might function tolerably well if responsible national policies were pursued in a framework of consultation and coordination.

STRATEGIES FOR COORDINATION

We consider it important, for the sake of regional and global economic integration, open trade and investment, and noninflationary growth, that the principal economic powers work together toward the long-term goal of more stable exchange rates. Achieving the "public goods" of open trade and global economic growth warrants such an effort, which will, in turn, create pressures for more consistent national macroeconomic policies. The alternative of a completely uncoordinated system, with nations inclined to pursue "beggar-thy-neighbor" policies, especially in depressed economic times, is likely to lead to trade protectionism and even to the re-emergence of controls on capital, and to split the global system into hostile national or regional entities.

Despite all the difficulties involved, therefore, **we favor an intensified effort by the G-7 and the IMF to achieve more stable exchange rates through macroeconomic policy coordination and, when necessary to prevent speculative runs, coordinated intervention by central banks in currency markets.** However, such efforts to stabilize rates, must be accompanied by a renewed determination to rectify inappropriate national policies. We doubt that the foundations of macroeconomic coordination, particularly the flexibility of fiscal policy in some countries, are strong enough to permit a system of formally fixed rates or target zones at the present time. However, we believe that if integration continues and the costs of inconsistent policies grow and manifest themselves in instability, mechanisms for the harmonization of both exchange rates and macroeconomic policies should be pursued.

Finally, we wish to emphasize that exchange rate stability is a means to economic prosperity, not an end in itself. The economic benefits of integration and specialization will, in the long term, avail us little if the world economy does not grow. Therefore, as efforts at policy coordination continue, policy makers must not lose sight of the fundamental goal of noninflationary growth that will raise living standards, (especially in the poorest countries), allow more nations to meet environmental goals, and reduce the political barriers to achieving social equity. In the context of macroeconomic policy, this means that attention must be given to the overall posture of fiscal and monetary policies in the major industrial countries. Consistency of those policies does not ensure that they are appropriate for growth. Consultation and coordination, therefore, should address the effects on global saving, investment, and growth of the fiscal and monetary policies of the G-7 in the aggregate in addition to the adjustment of structural imbalances among nations and regions.

CONCLUSIONS

The fundamental principles for the United States and other countries are clear. Fiscal policies should be conducted to produce more public saving than the United States and other countries have achieved lately; similarly, monetary policy should aim at steady, noninflationary economic growth. Fiscal and/or monetary policies will need to be adjusted to meet changing needs manifested in specific national problems, such as soaring German unification costs, Allied expenditures on the Gulf War, and recessions. But major industrial countries need to carry out economic policies

with their effects on the world economy taken explicitly into consideration.

There are no technical solutions to the economic problems the world is facing. What is most needed is the political will — the will of the United States and other countries to deal more effectively with their own problems and the will of all the major industrial countries to work together for a common end. With the diffusion of economic power, Japan, Germany, and the other major industrial countries must accept wider international responsibilities; but as the largest economic power in the world, the United States has a special responsibility to lay a foundation for cooperation by setting its own domestic economic policy in order. Only by being an effective model can the United States hope to lead other nations.

The most important challenge for economic cooperation in the years ahead will be to keep the world economy growing at a sustainable pace. With real economic growth, the serious problems of world debt, trade, and currency imbalances can be contained, and progress can be made toward their solution. The greatest change needed to preserve stability and growth is for the world economy to become the focus of policy formulation. Despite the resistance of traditional national politics and interest-group pressures, the development of stable monetary and fiscal policies in the major industrial countries has become vital to the economic well-being of every country.

DIRECTIONS FOR POLICY

1. In pursuit of the objective of stable economic growth, the United States should aim to increase its national saving rate ultimately to 8 percent of national income within a decade from its recent level of only 2 to 3 percent. The contribution that federal government can make in reaching that goal will be to reduce the structural budget deficit steadily in the years ahead, aiming at a budget surplus of 1 to 2 percent of national income within a decade.

2. Fiscal policy for stable growth should have a longer-run time horizon and should not be manipulated continuously for short-term stimulus or political purposes. Over time, such manipulation raises the nation's budget deficits, worsening the internal problems of saving, investment, and productivity growth, and the external problems of trade and payments deficits, currency weakness, and industrial competitiveness in world markets.

3. We recommend a continuing and intensified effort by the Group of Seven, working with the IMF and the OECD, to strengthen existing mechanisms for consultation and coordination on macroeconomic policies and exchange rates. Although a system of formally fixed rates seems premature under current political and institutional arrangements, inter-national economic integration will continue to increase the benefits of exchange rate stability, which should remain a major long-term objective.

4. We stress the importance of cooperative formulation of national macroeconomic policies among the EC, Japan, and the United States not only to facilitate a stable exchange rate system but, more important, to promote steady and noninflationary world growth. Structural adjustment to changes in international trade and investment patterns are more readily made in an environment of steady economic growth and rising employment and incomes.

C. GROWTH AND THE DEVELOPING WORLD[23]

The developing world — more than 140 nations that are home to 4 billion of the world's 5 billion people — will be a prime concern for the industrial world in the years ahead. The end of the cold war has given America and its partners an opportunity to reorder their priorities for international cooperation. The prospect of explosive population growth and deepening privation in many of these already impoverished countries must put healthy economic growth in the developing world near the top of the priority list.

The developing nations, most of which are less than thirty years old, are home to 80 percent of the world's population yet account for only 20 percent of world output and 17 percent of world trade. Although some of these countries have achieved remarkable progress, many remain in abject poverty; more than 1 billion citizens in developing countries live on less than $1 per day.

Citizens of these nations confront the disastrous effects of this poverty — precarious housing, malnutrition, inadequate access to basic health and medical facilities, and poor education — on a daily basis. For both humanitarian reasons and self-interest, the industrial world needs to help spur strong economic growth in the developing world by encouraging and abetting needed reforms, increasing and improving aid programs, and integrating these nations into a more open world economy. It is only through such economic growth that the citizens of developing countries will be able to enjoy healthy and productive lives, benefit from the increasing interdependence of the world economy, and achieve freedom and security.

THE INDUSTRIAL WORLD AND DEVELOPING NATIONS

Clearly, the industrial countries have a humanitarian concern about developing countries. There are also a number of problems facing the industrialized nations that can be solved only with the cooperation of the developing world. Illegal Mexican immigration into the United States and the influx of African refugees into Europe highlight the need for development. The current U.S. "war on drugs" will require governments in the developing world to crack down on drug producers in their countries. Improving the environment, containing international terrorism, restraining excessive population growth, preventing the spread of AIDS, and combating nuclear proliferation all require cooperation from the developing world. As William Draper, the United Nations Development Programme Administrator, has said, "This poverty [in developing countries] finds its way to the developed world, as pollution, drug exports, and terrorism. The desperately unemployed will also seek jobs where they exist, in the industrial nations as legal or illegal migrants."[24]

Until the 1950s, the U.S. economic stake in developing countries was quite limited in spite of some concentrated investment in primary exports. Developing nations were viewed as a source of primary products, host countries for minimal direct investment, and secondary markets for the export of manufactured goods.

By the early 1980s, this relationship had changed dramatically. In addition to continuing to serve as important sources of primary materials, these nations purchased almost 40 percent of U.S. exports.[25] This proportion exceeded, the proportion claimed by exports to the EC and Japan. In addition to gains from trade, our corporations became heavily reliant on operations in these countries. Developing nations also now serve as host countries for one-quarter of U.S. foreign direct investment.

The importance of developing countries to the health of the U.S. economy was underscored when these countries stopped growing in the early 1980s. Between 1981 and 1983, American exports to developing countries dropped by $25 billion (in constant 1987 dollars), substantially worsening our balance of trade and causing the loss of thousands of jobs in the United States. In the same period, U.S. annual income from direct investments in these countries fell by more than $7 billion.

More recently, in 1991, when industrialized countries were experiencing a slowdown, developing countries were one of the few growth markets for U.S. products. Developing countries increased their purchase of U.S. goods by 15 percent and accounted for nearly 80 percent of U.S. export growth. Figure 9 highlights our reliance on developing countries both as a source of U.S. imports and a market for our exports.

Sustained economic growth in these countries could provide vast new markets for exports of industrial country goods. The population of developing countries will increase by approximately 850 million people in the 1990s, more than the total current population of all the OECD countries. The United States sells more to Latin America than it does to Japan, with more than half of these sales going to Mexico. In fact, 70 percent of Mexican imports are from America; the comparable figure for Japan is 25 percent.[26] Moreover, a recent study by the Overseas Development Council projects that the United States will not be able to cut its trade deficit significantly through trade with the industrial world alone.[27] If the developing countries regain their growth

rates of the 1970s, U.S. exports to them could be as much as $30 billion higher within three years. This translates into as many as 600,000 new American jobs.[28] It is in developing countries, to the extent that their incomes rise, that demand for our goods will increase most rapidly.

THE IMPLICATIONS OF THE POPULATION EXPLOSION

The problem of poverty in the developing world is closely tied to demographic change. In most developing countries, the spread of new medical technologies has resulted in declines in death rates and an increase in average life expectancy from forty years to sixty years since 1950.[29] This remarkable achievement has not been accompanied by an equivalent decrease in fertility rates. The world population of 5.3 billion is projected to grow by almost 100 million in 1992 alone.

Estimates of future population growth are imprecise, but even the most optimistic pro-

Figure 9

U.S. Exports and Imports, Developing Countries
1965-1991

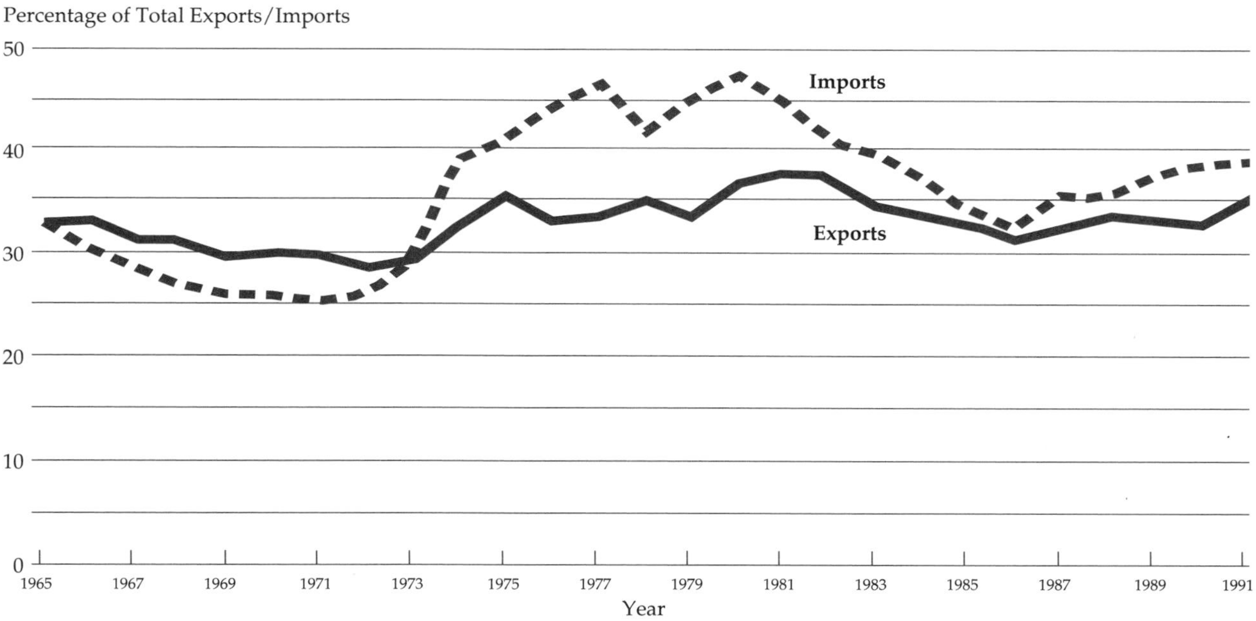

Percentage of Total Exports/Imports

SOURCE: Department of Commerce; Bureau of Economic Analysis, Bureau of the Census, Bureau of International Economic Policy and Research.

jections suggest that population will increase by 60 percent in the next generation. Figure 10 shows the World Bank's baseline, rapid, and low growth projections for world population; each has very different implications for world population in the coming decade. The low-growth projection is based on declines in fertility rates that are comparable to the recent experiences of Costa Rica and Mexico; the rapid-growth projection is consistent with the recent experiences of Sri Lanka and Turkey, and the baseline projection is somewhere in the middle. Although few demographers expect the world population to actually reach the high projected total of 23 billion people, the rapid-growth projection illustrates the potential for extreme population pressure if fertility rates are not reduced quickly, especially in the low-income countries of Africa and the Middle East that account for 85 to 90 percent of the differences between alternative projections.

Rapid population growth in low-income countries has adverse effects on economic development. It means societies have a disproportionate number of people in young age groups, which consume but do not produce and create wealth. This burden of dependency reduces domestic saving, making it even more difficult to invest and raise per capita incomes.

The reduction of fertility rates to a more sustainable rate requires a multi-faceted approach. One reason parents in the Third World have such large families is to help provide support during sickness and old age. Any means to systematically increase incomes would remove some of this motivation. Reducing infant mortality will have similar effects in lowering birth rates, as parents realize that more of their children will survive to adulthood.

Improving the economic independence of women through better education and labor force participation has also been shown to reduce fertility rates. When no women are enrolled in secondary education, the average woman has seven children; where as few as 40 percent of women have a secondary education, the average is only three, even after controlling for a variety of factors including income.[30] Moreover, women with greater edu-

cational opportunities raise healthier families, have better-educated children, and are more productive both at home and at work.

The extension of family-planning programs is another important strategy to reduce fertility rates. Between 1980 and 1990, contraceptive use in developing countries increased to a rate of 49 percent from 40 percent. However, in some countries such as Bolivia, Ghana, and Togo, more than 35 percent of couples cannot obtain the contraceptives they desire. For the baseline projection to be met, the rate would have to increase another 7 percent by the year 2000, and reach 61 percent by the year 2010. This would imply increasing annual expenditures on family planning by $3 billion to a level of nearly $8 billion (in 1990 prices) by 2000; the slow-growth projection would require a further $3 billion commitment to reach a total of $14 billion.

During the 1980s, the U.S. curtailed funding for family planning programs and

Figure 10

World Population Projections
Under Different Fertility Trends

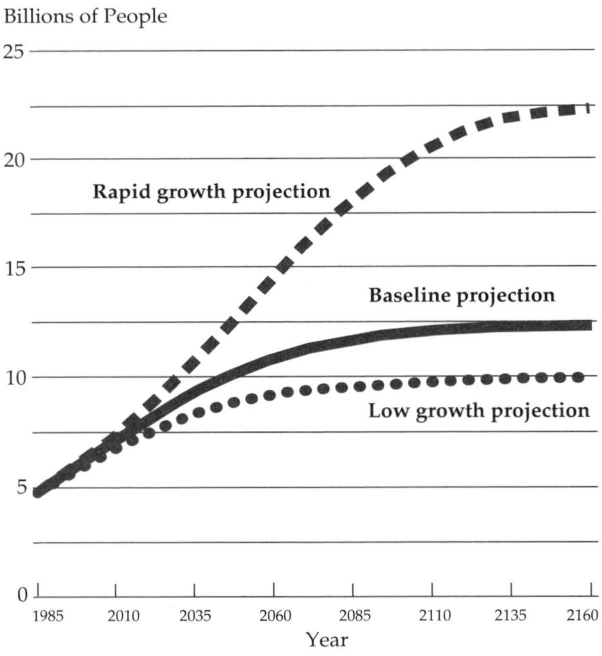

SOURCE: World Bank

withdrew support for major international organziations such as the U.N. Population Fund and the International Planned Parenthood Federation. As a result, international family planning funding is falling behind the increase in demand for services in the developing world. **CED strongly recommends that the United States reverse its retreat from this issue and bring the issue of family planning onto the international agenda, where it has been ignored of late at events such as the UN-sponsored environmental summit in Rio de Janeiro.** The industrialized countries should actively promote the education of women and the provision of family-planning services in order to forestall severe population pressures and their adverse effects on both national living standards and the environment.

THE RECENT ECONOMIC EXPERIENCE OF DEVELOPING COUNTRIES

In the 1980s, external economic shocks and poor domestic policies stopped growth in many developing countries. These countries were rocked by worldwide recession, declines in world trade, steep decreases in the prices of their basic export commodities that severely damaged their terms of trade, and a sharp increase in real interest rates. When these external shocks were combined with imprudent debt accumulation, irresponsible domestic macroeconomic policies, and mismanaged microeconomic policies, the result was the debt crisis that struck much of the developing world. Private lenders, in turn, almost completely shut off flows of foreign capital to them. By the end of 1986 more than forty countries in Latin America, Africa, and elsewhere were suffering through severe economic stagnation or contraction.

The Asian countries, especially those in East Asia, had pursued sound domestic economic policies were able to survive the macroeconomic instability and continued their growth. Table 1, however, reveals that the 1980s were the "lost decade" for the rest of the developing world. The sub-Saharan African countries and the Latin American countries that were overwhelmed by massive debts actually saw declines in their output; countries such as Zambia, Nigeria, Bolivia, and Venezuela experienced declines in output similar in size to the United States' loss of output in the Great Depression.

DOMESTIC POLICY, CAPITAL, AND GROWTH

Since developing countries had such sharply divergent experiences in recent years, it is important to understand what factors separate those that experienced growth from those that did not. In 1990, the World Bank indicated that the growth of some nations could be traced to the rate of investment in those nations.[31]

Determining why some developing countries have been able to invest more in their productive capacity is central to understanding how to help future development.

One simple conclusion is that war stops productive investment and, in turn, development. Of the thirty-six countries that saw their incomes decline over the last twenty-five years, almost all were involved in major military conflicts. Even though the Middle East is considered home to constant strife, Africa's war fatality rate is three times higher. In the last thirty years, this prolonged warring has translated into 7 million war-related deaths.[32] The constant conflict has undermined the ability of many African countries to provide adequate basic services to their citizens, which has indirectly led to the death of millions more. For example, sub-Saharan African governments on average spend four times as much on the military as on health care, and their military budgets are as large as their expenditures on education. By comparison, in East Asia, spending on both health and education greatly exceeds military budgets. Military spending in the developing world as a whole declined by 20 percent from 1984 to 1990, but in the poorest regions, such as South Asia and sub-Saharan Africa, it has not declined.[33] These military expenditures divert scarce resources from development while the wars that they sustain deter both domestic and foreign investment.

By itself, avoiding war does not guarantee that a country will be able to attract the necessary investments in its future. Lawrence Summers, the chief economist of the World Bank, suggests four principles for domestic policies that, in the absence of war, will encourage growth in the developing nations.[34]

First, sustainable fiscal deficits and realistic exchange rates are the foundations of development. In many developing countries, large budget deficits accommodated by expansionary monetary policies have resulted in high inflation rates, overvalued exchange rates, and huge current-account deficits. The budget deficits soak up significant portions of domestic savings and foreign funds that could otherwise be channeled to productive investment in the private sector. Inflation induces higher real exchange rates and reduces foreign exchange earnings by lowering total exports. Furthermore, overall instability promotes capital flight, further reducing the amount of capital that is available for investment.

Second, governments must provide a business environment that is favorable, not hostile, to private ventures. Such an environment requires that market forces determine prices without price controls or large subsidies to certain goods such as energy and agricultural products. Moreover, governments need to welcome rather than discourage direct investment from foreign enterprises.

Third, governments must cease producing private goods and services. Public managers are often prevented from reducing labor inputs, a step often necessary for competitive performance. And procurement policies are all too often based on politics. The United Nations estimates that if developing countries were to privatize inefficient public enterprises and reduce military expenditures, they would have an extra $50 billion a year for development purposes, almost the size of all official development assistance (ODA), the largest category for direct transfers to the developing world.[35]

Table 1

Growth of Real Per Capita Income, 1960-1990
(average annual Percentage change)

Group	1960-1970	1970-1980	1980-1990
Industrial countries	4.1	2.3	2.3
Developing countries	3.3	2.5	1.6
Sub-Saharan Africa	0.6	0.9	-0.9
Asia and the Pacific	2.5	3.1	5.1
East Asia	3.6	4.6	6.3
South Asia	1.4	1.1	3.1
Middle East and North Africa	6.0	3.1	-2.5
Latin America and the Caribbean	2.5	3.1	-0.5
Europe	4.9	4.4	1.2
Eastern Europe	5.2	5.4	0.9
Developing Countries Weighted by Population	3.9	3.7	2.2

NOTE: Totals do not include the former USSR

SOURCE: World Bank 1992.

Fourth, countries should provide basic infrastructure and investment in human capital necessary to attract private investment. Countries need to invest in good roads and communications systems to facilitate the conduct of commerce. In addition, to attract capital, countries must provide adequate funding for educational institutions, health care, and environmental protection, which contribute to a healthy, high-quality labor force. A number of studies have revealed a link between improvements in human capital and economic growth. One study of 88 countries found that an increase from 20 percent to 30 percent in the literacy rate was associated with an increase in real GDP of between 8 percent and 16 percent and improvements in nutrition and health have been shown to account for 20 percent to 30 percent of per capita income growth.[36]

In the past decade, Asian countries, to varying degrees, pursued policies that were consistent with these four principles, especially in terms of investment in human capital. When the external shocks of the 1980s came along, they continued to attract investment and sustain growth. While Asian countries were successfully pursuing these policies, most other developing countries, particularly in Latin America and sub-Saharan Africa, did not make these adjustments and saw their economic positions falter as foreign lending dried up.[37]

DEBT AND GROWTH

Mexico's 1982 announcement that it would have to suspend repayment of the principal of its loans was the first event to call attention to the Latin American debt crisis that has had dramatic effects for both the industrial and developing countries. The size of the aggregate Latin American debt, relative to bank capital, threatened the stability of banking systems in the industrial countries. At the same time, the resulting restrictions on capital flows caused declines in real output, the enactment of economic austerity plans, social problems, and political battles over economic policy in the developing countries.

In the wake of Mexico's announcement, the IMF, World Bank, and the central banks of a few key countries mapped out a controversial strategy: They agreed that the debtors should receive new loans so that they could continue to pay the interest on the debt. The new loans enabled the Latin American countries to introduce IMF approved economic reforms to restore private sector confidence and gave the money-center banks time to build up enough capital reserves to absorb losses caused by loans.

This strategy was modified by the proposals of both U.S. Treasury Secretary Baker in 1985, and in 1989 expanded and further refined by Secretary Brady. The revised plan acknowledged the deleterious effects that large debt loads were having on growth and attempted to reduce these loads through longer maturities, lower interest rates, and/or debt for equity swaps that were often linked to privatization programs. Since 1990, Mexico, Costa Rica, the Phillipines, Uruguay, and Venezuela have all agreed to Brady debt reduction plans, and in 1992 Argentina and Brazil reached outline agreements. When these two deals are completed, more than 90 percent of the commercial bank debt of large debtor countries will have been addressed by debt reduction agreements.

These efforts appear to have enabled these nations to resume growth. Latin America once again has had access to new private capital; private capital flows to Latin countries have jumped from $5 billion in 1989 to more than $40 billion in 1991. While the Latin America countries are not guaranteed success in the future, they are on the right path and their debt crisis has passed. Similarly, the international financial community has also escaped the dangers it once faced.

However, there are two other looming debt crises. The first is occuring in the poorest countries of the world, primarily in sub-Saharan Africa, that have had shrinking per capita incomes in the last decade. The majority of these countries have received support through concessional lending, debt forgiveness, and debt restructuring tied to economic reforms, from the multilateral institutions and the industrialized countries. Despite this support, these countries are currently only servicing about half of their repayment obligations.

If these countries are to have the capital necessary to realize the economic growth they desperately need, their debt servicing obligations must be reduced. Due to their weak economies, they have never been able to secure private financing and are not likely to be creditworthy soon. They will have to continue to rely on official sources as their primary provider of capital. While their debts are quite large relative to their incomes, they are small relative to the industrialized nations' output. The World Bank estimates that a doubling of total finacial transfers to these countries would cost $10 billion, or less than 1 percent of annual world defense spending.[38]

The second looming debt crisis is in the former Soviet Union. The CIS currently has $70 billion in debt, that it is currently incapable of repaying. Clearly the CIS will have to undertake vigorous economic reforms, but even with these reforms the individual economies will need temporary relief from their debt loads. As the Latin American crisis revealed, such relief will require the participation of the industrialized countries and the multilateral institutions.

ACCESS TO FOREIGN CAPITAL

Although a substantial portion of the capital invested in middle-income developing countries is financed by domestic saving, developing countries are still quite dependent on external capital from two primary sources: private capital and official foreign assistance. The low-income countries generally do not have access to private capital markets, but they do rely on official foreign assistance and trade.

THE SUPPLY OF PRIVATE CAPITAL.

Private capital generally moves to developing countries in the form of either foreign direct investment or international bank lending at market rates. Figure 11 reveals that during the 1970s and 1980s, the flow of private capital to developing countries followed three separate trends: In 1970, net private resource flows to developing countries from countries on the Development Assistance Committee (DAC) of the OECD stood at $26 billion (in 1987 constant dollars); but by 1981, this had

more than tripled to $78 billion.[39] In 1982, the Latin American debt crisis spurred a precipitous decline in net private transfers; it reached bottom at $30 billion in net transfers from all countries in 1986. A number of factors caused this decline, including higher oil prices, the jump in real interest rates, the decline in commodity prices, and the worldwide recession. Because the flows of capital in the late 1970s and early 1980s were larger than the developing countries could productively absorb, they accumulated an enormous debt load without making the productive investment needed to service it.

This decrease in capital flows was an especially heavy blow to the middle-income developing countries, most notably Latin American nations, that relied more heavily on private sources of external finance. After the 1985-1987 period, a recovery in the amount of private capital raised resource flows from the entire world to $45 billion in 1989, and returned private transfers from DAC countries to the level of the early 1970s.

Figure 11

Net Private Resource Flows to Developing Countries
From DAC Countries, 1970-89 and World, 1978-89

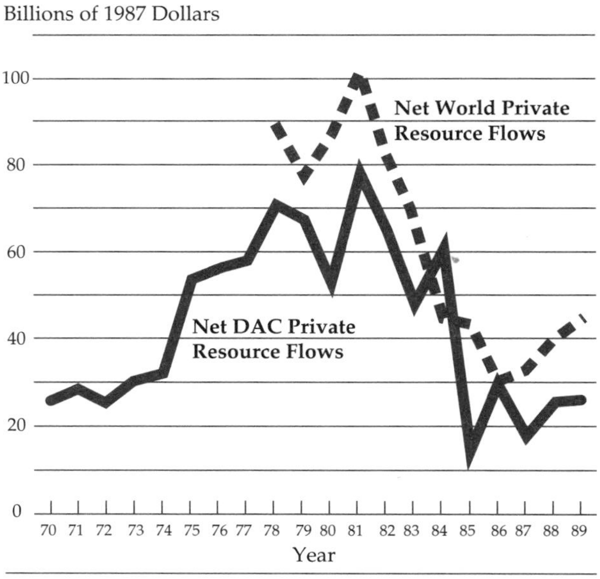

Billions of 1987 Dollars

SOURCE: Organization for Economic Co-operation and Development

51

Since 1989, countries such as Chile, Mexico, and Uruguay, have implemented macroeconomic reforms and reduced their debt loads through Brady aggreements. These changes have restored the confidence of the private sector and have led to inflows of foreign capital and a resurgence of economic growth.[40] Between 1990 and 1991, for instance, foreign direct investment in Mexico nearly tripled to $12.3 billion, and foreign lending increased by almost 35 percent. When sound economic policies are followed and debt is reduced, the private sector will provide both loans and foreign direct investment.

OFFICIAL FOREIGN ASSISTANCE

Another source of external capital for developing countries is foreign assistance, which is especially important for low-income countries that do not have access to private capital and that have very low domestic saving rates.

Multilateral Assistance. In the 1980s, net transfers to the developing countries from the multilateral institutions declined sharply in response to the financial crises in the developing world.[41] In 1983, IMF net transfers to developing countries totaled $7.6 billion, but by 1987 had reversed to -$7.9 billion. Although IMF intervention is primarily intended to aid in short term balance of payments problems, the decline in net transfers served to withdraw money from the developing countries at the same time that the private sector had withdrawn.

While the World Bank increased the average size of its loans, the number of them significantly declined. Its net transfers declined from a high of $5.2 billion in 1984 to -$0.7 billion in 1988, before rebounding to $0.7 billion in 1990. This decline took place at the same time that flows from the private sector declined. The World Bank, established to transfer rich nations' savings to poorer ones to finance development, relies on two major lending organs. One arm, the International Bank for Reconstruction and Development (IBRD), provides loans at interest rates that move in concert with private market rates. The other arm, the International Development Association (IDA) provides loans on concessional terms with longer repayment periods (forty years plus a ten-year grace period) to countries with per capita GNP below $700. Even with more than one billion people living in absolute poverty, IDA only accounts for 20 percent to 30 percent of the total World Bank lending. **Greater U.S. support for increases in the size of IDA replenishment would improve the poorest countries' access to capital.** Although the net transfer figures seem to reflect a significant decline in resource transfers to the developing world, this figure can be misleading; it includes the repayment of loans from countries that have experienced rapid growth and are no longer borrowing from the Bank.

Bilateral Assistance. Of the different forms of bilateral aid, ODA is the most important to the developing countries. Defined as development assistance provided unilaterally by a national government to another country, it can take a number of different forms, including cash grants, debt forgiveness, technical assistance, food, and loans at below-market rates. Figure 12 reveals that from 1970 to 1980, the provision of ODA to the developing countries grew by 50 percent, from $31 billion (in constant 1987 dollars) to $50 billion. This increase was driven largely by a substantial increase in giving from the oil producing countries. From 1980 to 1989, ODA held constant at slightly under $50 billion. As the OPEC countries reaped smaller oil profits, their giving declined and the industrialized countries stepped up their aid.

The DAC nations did not contribute equally to the growth in aid.[42] Although the Scandinavian countries all greatly increased their assistance as a percentage of GNP, other countries such as the United States and Australia decreased their giving. In total, DAC countries increased their ODA from .34 percent of GNP to .35 percent, about half the level of the United Nations' target of 0.7 percent of GNP. Approximately 80 percent of the shortfall is the responsibility of the United States and Japan. Evidence suggests that this aid is also not directed at the most pressing needs: 1) The richest 40 percent of the developing world's popula-

Figure 12

Net Official Development Assistance Flows to Developing Countries, 1970-89

World Total and DAC Countries, 1970-89

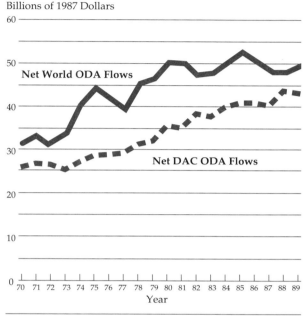

Billions of 1987 Dollars

SOURCE: Organization for Economic Co-operation and Development

tion receives more than double the aid per capita that the poorest 40 percent receives. 2) Countries with high military expenditures are given roughly twice the amount of aid as countries that spend more modestly. 3) Only 6.5 percent of bilateral ODA is provided for basic human concerns like education, primary health care, safe drinking water, family planning, and nutrition programs (the comparable figure for multilateral organizations is only 10 percent).[43]

While the U.S. foreign development assistance outlays are included in these figures, U.S. funding deserves special attention. Since World War II, the U.S. economic assistance program has sought to achieve a wide range of goals: advancing U.S. strategic and political interests, promoting economic development in the Third World, meeting emergency needs in the world's poorest countries, and expanding U.S. exports. Although the Foreign Assistance Act of 1973 and the 1978 Humphrey Bill attempted to focus foreign aid more explicitly on "basic human needs" (i.e., improving the living conditions of the "poorest of the poor"), recent foreign aid, has more often been directed toward security objectives.

Table 2 reveals that since 1970 there have been three major shifts in U.S. assistance pat-

Table 2

U.S. Foreign Assistance, Fiscal Years 1970 to 1993
Billions of 1993 dollars and Percent of Total

Fiscal Years	Multilateral Contributions	Bilateral Development Aid	Bilateral Security Aid	Total Aid Billions of 1993 Dollars	Total Aid As a percentage of GDP
1970-1973	4.8	34.5	60.7	109.4	.718
1974-1977	9.0	36.0	55.0	81.9	.457
1978-1981	12.1	34.0	53.9	79.5	.422
1982-1985	9.4	29.6	61.0	83.8	.417
1986-1989	8.1	31.9	60.0	73.3	.320
1990-1993(a)	8.3	39.3	52.4	65.9	.274

(a) 1992 numbers are estimated and 1993 numbers are the Administration's request

SOURCE: Congressional Research Service

terns. From the Vietnam War through the 1978-1981 period, there was a general change in emphasis from security-related aid to multilateral and bilateral aid for development. During the 1980s defense buildup, the priorities of the aid program were reversed, and security again became a priority. At the same time that other sources of capital (primarily private capital) were drying up, the United States also cut back on development aid. Since 1990, there has been a mild shift toward greater development aid, although assistance directed toward security still accounts for more than half of the total.

Table 2 also reveals our weak support for multilateral institutions and our relative preference for bilateral aid. Since bilateral development and security aid account for more than 90 percent of total foreign aid, it is worth examining what countries are the largest recipients. Figure 13 shows that when recipients of U.S. aid are divided into income categories, low-income countries receive the smallest amount of money on a per capita basis, and high-income and low-middle-income countries receive the most.[44,45] These trends are ocurring at the same time that the low-income countries are being overwhelmed by the massive debt loads they face. It is clear that the allocation of development aid is not primarily motivated by development and humanitarian concerns.

Changes in the assistance program must be viewed within the larger perspective of significantly declining total aid in real terms. In the last twenty years, there has been a gradual decline in the size of the U.S. aid program. By 1992, foreign assistance spending had fallen to approximately half its 1972 level. As a percentage of GDP, the drop has been steeper, from 0.76 percent in 1972 to 0.29 percent in 1992. Earlier in the post World War II period, U.S. foreign assistance had accounted for 2 to 3 percent of GNP in the late 1940s and approximately 1 percent in the late 1950s. Although the United States provides the second-largest amount of ODA to developing countries in absolute terms, it provides the second-smallest amount as a percentage of its GNP. Furthermore, in recent years the U.S.

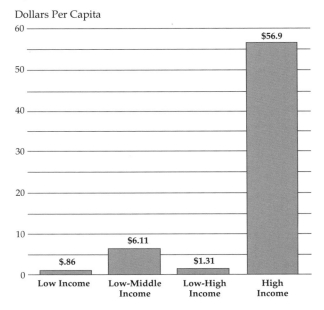

Figure 13

Total U.S. Foreign Assistance
By Income Level of Recipient Country, 1991

Dollars Per Capita

SOURCE: Agency for International Development

share of the total foreign economic assistance provided by DAC countries has fallen to an all-time low.[46]

Although bilateral assistance is an important tool for achieving U.S. objectives, multilateral aid has a number of unique advantages. It can help to promote a stable international economic environment, and it is more effective per dollar for the United States because costs are shared with other countries. Moreover, it generally places a greater emphasis on development goals. **For these reasons, CED encourages a greater reliance on multilateral institutions, and, in particular, the World Bank, which should remain the primary vehicle for channelling official capital to the developing countries.**

The U.S. government has traditionally maintained that judging the amount of aid a country gives by the percentage of GNP fails to take into account the other ways (e.g., defense expenditures) in which nations contribute to international political and economic order. As high U.S defense expenditures decline and threats to international stability become more localized, this argument will become less persuasive.

The demise of the Soviet Union provides the United States with an excellent opportunity to reorder its priorities for economic assistance. **In the new global environment, we should give more emphasis to economic need**. There will still be a role for aid designed to meet other goals such as domestic political reforms, environmentally sustainable growth, and nonproliferation of weapons. Nevertheless in the post cold war world, the importance of these different objectives has undoubtedly changed and the United States must react to these changes.

TRADE AND THE DEVELOPING WORLD

In addition to private capital markets and official assitance, trade is an important source of the foreign exchange. Developing country exports (excluding oil) provide almost ten times as much foreign exchange as the total flows of bilateral and multilateral financial assistance from the United States, Japan, and Western Europe. Although developing countries' domestic policies (e.g., exchange rates, levels of protection, and other interventions) are primarily responsible for the success or failure of individual nations in world trade, the industrial nations have an important role to play. **The most important step in helping developing countries is for the industrial countries to create an environment of steady noninflationary growth that sustains imports from the developing world.**

The trade policies of the industrial world also directly affect developing countries' ability to export. As the industrial nations have raised trade barriers in the past decade, many developing countries have reduced their barriers to trade, either unilaterally or as a condition for World Bank and IMF loans. If developing countries were granted unrestricted access to industrial country markets, they would gain $40 billion in foreign exchange through additional exports, almost as much

as they receive in total aid. According to the World Bank, these barriers translate into a reduction of $75 billion, or 3 percent, of the developing world's GNP.

For example, subsidies and protection granted to the farmers of OECD countries, particularly in the EC, severely damage the export prospects of the developing world. Assistance to farmers through supply-management programs, price supports, and direct payments raises the production of agricultural products in industrialized countries and lowers world prices. The result is that farmers in developing countries, who may be lower-cost producers, cannot sell their goods in the developed world. In addition, approximately one-third of the agricultural exports from the developing countries are subject to quantitative import restrictions, such as the limits on exports of sugar to the United States and rice to Japan.

Through the Multifibre Arrangement, the industrial countries have set up quotas (also known as voluntary export restraints and orderly marketing agreements) that limit the exports of textiles and apparel from low-cost producers. Removal of all Multifibre Arrangement quotas would increase total exports of clothing and textiles from developing countries by approximately $24 billion a year. Unlike tariffs, which an exporting country can overcome by increasing its productivity and lowering its prices, quantitative restrictions place an absolute limit on imports. These policies undermine the effectiveness of IMF and World Bank policies that push developing countries to adopt more realistic (and often lower) exchange rates because they make exports insensitive to prices.

These trade restrictions preserve jobs and incomes in industrial economies at a very high cost. The annual cost of the Multifibre Agreement to American consumers has been estimated to be $25 billion at wholesale prices and $40 billion at retail, and sugar quotas cost an extra $1.9 billion.[47] On a per-job basis, the costs are enormous. In Canada, for example, every dollar earned by workers who keep their jobs because of the Multifibre Arrangement costs society approximately $70; in the United States,

THE DEVELOPING COUNTRIES AND THE ENVIRONMENT[48]

Both the expected population increases and needed economic growth in the developing world have the potential to place severe strains on the natural environment. The World Bank projects that world output will be 3.5 times its current level in 2030. If environmental pollution and degradation were to rise in proportion to output, dangerous levels of pollution and damage would result. Ultimately, the earth's resources and ability to absorb pollution may place a limit on growth. Many contend that the world must strike a balance between the twin goals of growth and protection of the environment. (Others, we believe unrealistically, contend that this is a false choice and that no such trade-offs need to be made.) Figure 14 makes clear that growth can affect the environment in a number of ways.

- Some indicators of environmental stress, such as the percentage of the population without safe water and the percentage of urban populations without adequate sanitation, *decline as incomes increase.* As incomes rise, people do not have to devote all their attention to survival and can invest in public services and conservation.

- Other environmental indicators, such as the urban concentrations of particulate matter and sulfur dioxide, *initially worsen but then improve as incomes rise.* Most types of air and water pollution fit into this category, as do some types of deforestation and encroachment on natural habitats. These environmental problems impose definite costs on a particular area; when the costs become large enough relative to their income, countries often make a conscious decision to introduce policies to address the situation.

- Some indicators of environmental stress, such as municipal wastes per capita and carbon dioxide emissions per capita, have tended to *continually worsen as incomes increase.* Two factors cause these declines: 1) The costs of abatement are relatively high, and 2) The social costs are incorrectly perceived to be very low because they are not borne directly by the polluters. For example, reductions in carbon dioxide emissions would require substantial investments in pollution abatement devices, and the potential harm from these emissions is spread across the globe and would only minimally harm the actual polluters. Governments have been very reluctant to address these problems, and businesses and individuals have very few incentives to reduce these types of pollution.[49]

The improvement in some indicators as incomes rise does not occur automatically. It requires deliberate action by governments to promote these improvements. Countries at similar income levels may have very different environmental conditions because of deliberate policies. In addition, technological progress has enabled countries to develop in a "cleaner" way than was possible in the past at any given level of income.

In order to develop in a cleaner way, nations need to include the external benefits and social costs in any cost-benefit analysis.[50] The social costs can be better recognized in three key areas:
1) There are a number of policies that are good for increasing growth and also good for the environment. The four principles for domestic growth described above all benefit the natural environment in that they allow for the spread of new technologies, provide an educated work force for implementing them, remove subsidies that promote overconsumption of energy, and clarify property rights so that forests, pasturelands, or fishing areas are not overused.
2) Not all environmental problems will be cured by growth; in fact, some require changes in behavior. Generally, these either provide incentives for actors to efficiently change their behavior or place quantitative restrictions on some activity. Examples of market-based rules include fuel taxes, carbon taxes, and congestion charges; quantitative controls have been used to relieve pressures on land usage. CED believes market-based policies that attempt to internalize the social costs of activities should be used to the greatest extent possible.
3) Public investment projects should assess the environmental effects of any new project. International and national agencies have had poor records of successfully measuring the environmental impact of their projects.[51]

The explosion in world population, largely concentrated in poor countries, presents serious challenges to the environment. It is in the interest of the United States to pursue policies that help increase incomes in developing countries, including continued support for an open global trading and investment system. Assistance to poorer, resource-intensive industrial countries in making the transition to mature market economies will foster better energy use and environmental protection. Of course, the extent to which technological improvement can counter the strains of increasing population is open to question. This underscores the need for family planning in developing countries, not only as a means of improving their prospects for economic growth but also as a contribution to better environmental conditions.

Figure 14

Environmental Indicators at Different Country Income Levels

Population without safe water

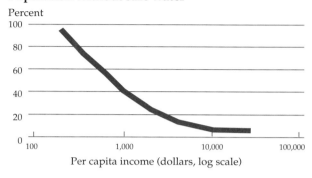

Percent

Per capita income (dollars, log scale)

Urban population without adequate sanitation

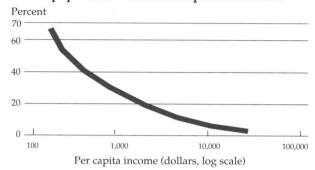

Percent

Per capita income (dollars, log scale)

Urban concentrations of particulate matter

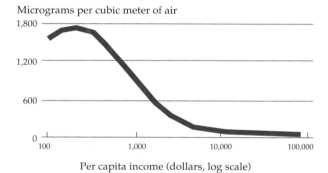

Micrograms per cubic meter of air

Per capita income (dollars, log scale)

Urban concentrations of sulfur dioxide

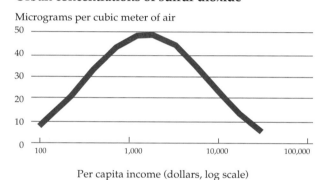

Micrograms per cubic meter of air

Per capita income (dollars, log scale)

Municipal wastes per capita

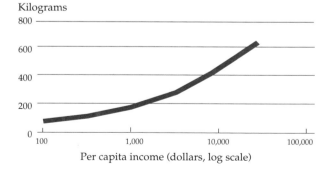

Kilograms

Per capita income (dollars, log scale)

Carbon dioxide emissions per capita[a]

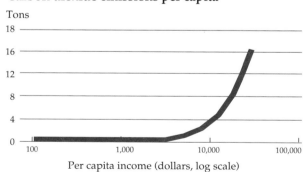

Tons

Per capita income (dollars, log scale)

NOTE: Estimates are based on cross-country regression analysis of data from the 1980s.

a. Emissions are from fossil fuels

SOURCES: Shafik and Bandyopadhyay, background paper; World Bank data.

protectionism in the steel industry costs consumers $114,000 a year for each job saved.[52] **CED supports efforts to reduce such inefficient protection, and urges continued U.S. leadership for a successful resolution of the Uruguay Round.**

Another area of concern for some developing countries is the movement to regional trading blocs such as the single European market and NAFTA that may reduce trade barriers between participating industrial countries while leaving higher barriers on the rest of the world. As the industrial economies have begun to develop trading blocs, many developing countries (particularly in Asia and Africa) have been left to fend for themselves.

The effect of these blocs on the developing countries depends on whether the trade-promoting effects of faster regional growth outweigh the trade-diverting effects of discriminatory external barriers. Gains for developing countries would come if the blocs reduced inefficiencies, causing GDP to increase and spurring greater imports. Some developing countries would suffer if trade is diverted from a lower-cost interregional pattern to a higher-cost intraregional one. The most damaging possibility, however, is that the blocs will actually raise barriers to the rest of the world. Such a move would be disastrous to the developing countries reliant on trade with the industrial economies for foreign exchange.

CED applauds the Administration's liberalization trade with Mexico through NAFTA as the first step in its plans for a Western Hemisphere free trade zone enunciated in the Enterprise for the America initiative. However, the United States should not limit these trade agreements to countries in its geographic region, but rather offer to open negotiations with any interested countries. The inclusion of less developed countries in liberalized trading arrangements will aid both the United States and its new partners. Conversely, the lack of European interest in including sub-Saharan African countries as well as the former Eastern bloc countries is detrimental both to the EC and developing countries.

Trade and aid are complementary ways of providing developing countries with the foreign exchange that they need. But there is an essential difference between the two: Aid entails a sacrifice by the donor; trade is mutually beneficial to both sides of the transaction. When a country liberalizes trade or removes a barrier to imports, it helps not only the foreign exporter but its own producers and consumers as well.

DIRECTIONS FOR POLICY

1. The industrialized countries should not mistakenly conclude that the end of the cold war ends their need for concern about developing countries. Rather, they need to acknowledge the range of interests — economic, political, strategic, humanitarian, and environmental — that they have in promoting economic development in the developing world. Sustained economic growth in the industrial countries remains the necessary condition for growth and improved living standards in the developing countries.

2. In addition to a healthy global economic environment, two other factors are necessary for sustained economic growth in the developing countries. First, they must pursue sound macro and micro-economic policies so that their economies will efficiently allocate resources and gain the confidence of the private sector. Second, excessive debt can serve as a very real drag on economic growth, even when a country is pursuing sound economic policies. The industrialized countries should continue to make foreign assistance conditional on sound economic policies, and help the CIS and severely indebted low-income countries to reduce debt to levels where they will be able to experience economic growth.

3. The United States should push the issue of family planning onto the international agenda, where it has been ignored recently. The industrialized countries should actively promote the education of women and the provision of family-planning services in order to forestall severe population pressures, with their adverse effects on both economic growth and the environment.

4. The demise of the Soviet Union presents the United States with an opportunity to reorder its priorities and rethink policies for foreign economic assistance. First, there will still be a need for bilateral aid, but the new world situation provides the United States with the opportunity to place a greater emphasis on multilateral aid. A simple way to accomplish this goal would be through a greater reliance on the multilateral organizations in general, particularly the World Bank. Second, the United States still devotes less than half of its foreign assistance to development aid. The end of the cold war provides the United States with an opportunity to increase both the relative and absolute size of development-related aid. Third, the United States should reverse its recent trend and at least maintain, and if possible increase, the share of its GDP going to development assistance.

5. Further trade liberalization will significantly strengthen the economies of the developing world. Therefore, the United States should continue its vigorous efforts at trade liberalization in GATT, especially in agriculture, textiles, and other labor-intensive sectors, where developing countries have a comparative advantage. Multilateral agreements through GATT should be the primary focus of U.S. efforts. The United States, however, should also work for free-trade zones with any interested developing country regardless of geographical location.

CHAPTER 4

IMPROVING AMERICA'S CAPACITY TO LEAD

Although the threats to America's competitive position are often overstated, concern about the future of U.S. leadership is not entirely unfounded. In a world where the ability to lead is increasingly dependent on a nation's economic prowess, indicators suggest that the U.S. economy is not healthy. Although productivity growth does not receive the front-page headlines that Japanese trade barriers do, it is quite simply the most important long-run determinant of a country's economic strength and living standards. Figure 15 reveals that measured by this critical economic indicator, the economy has struggled since the early 1970s.

This slowdown has been reflected in decreases in the growth rate of wages for all Americans. As Table 3 demonstrates, the growth in real compensation per hour, which

includes fringe benefits such as health care, has significantly slowed since 1973 and is virtually unchanged from its 1979 level. Average hourly wages, which exclude fringe benefits, have actually declined at an annual rate of 0.4 percent since 1973, leaving the current average hourly wage at approximately the 1965 level, after adjusting for inflation.

At the same time, the United States has failed to invest more in its future productive capability. U.S. investment in capital has fallen far behind both that of our competitors and our own past performance: U.S. net fixed investment, expressed as a percentage of our net national product, has fallen to half its 1950 level. U.S. spending on civilian research and development, expressed as a percentage of GDP, has lagged far behind that of our major competitors. Even the caliber of the new Ameri-

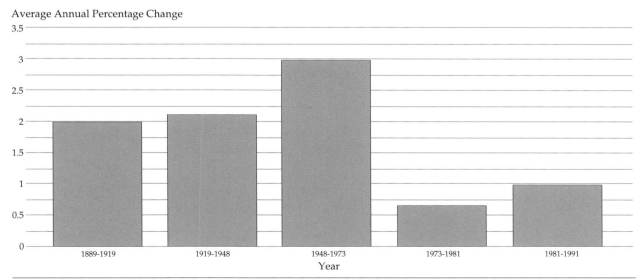

Figure 15

Long-Term Trends in U.S. Output Per Hour Growth
1889-1991

Average Annual Percentage Change

SOURCE: Kendrick (1991) and Bureau of Labor Statistics

can work force has slipped; recent studies place American students well behind their peers in other countries.

As these disturbing trends jeopardize the economic base of U.S. international leadership, another closely related dynamic threatens our more intangible leadership qualities. According to most estimates, the gap between the income levels of rich and poor in the United States has been widening for the last twenty years. This trend, coupled with increasingly apparent symbols of U.S. inability to address its most pressing domestic needs, imperils a second component of U.S. international strength: its moral capital. Other nations have long looked to the United States as the paragon of a free society, in which all citizens have an equal opportunity for success. With the deterioration of our public institutions and the rise of a permanent underclass, we have lost some of the international respect that has served as a remarkable tool for persuasion and inspiration.

Despite these danger signs, in an interdependent world full of threats to its unity and stability, the United States still has a crucial role to play, which we have called *a rallier of nations*. But America needs to strengthen its economy and society if it is to play that role successfully and enable its citizens to achieve their aspirations.

New developments in the global economy have changed the nature of competitive advantage. Raw natural resources, once the chief determinant of wealth, now mean little without the ability to make full and productive use of them. In fact, several of the world's richest nations — Japan, for example — are notably resource poor. Advances in transportation and reductions of trade barriers have rendered geography increasingly irrelevant. Greater international security has diminished the commercial importance of military strength. In the new global economy, constant innovation and the know-how to convert innovation to productive use will be the foundations of economic growth.

A competitive America must raise productivity growth, and this requires increases in both private and public investment. We define investment broadly as the commitment of resources to activities that raise future output rather than to current consumption—the production of "seed corn" rather than bread. In practice, investment may encompass a triad of interdependent activities that increase the stock of physical, technological, and human capital.

The best measure of the fruitfulness of such investment is the trend of total-factor productivity in the United States. *Total-factor productivity*, unlike the more frequently cited measure *labor productivity*, attempts to take into account all inputs into the production of goods and services and provides a more accurate measure of the importance of various inputs.[1] Different studies have shown that about half

Table 3

Select Measures of Worker Wages and Compensation, 1948 to 1991
(average annual rates of change, percent)

	1948-73	1973-1991
Real compensation per hour (a)	3.2	0.6
Average real hourly wages (b)	2.3	-0.4

NOTE: Growth rate calculated based on CPI-U-X1 price deflator after 1966.

(a) Includes payroll workers in all industries.

(b) Includes only production and non-supervisory workers on nonagricultural payrolls.

SOURCE: U.S. Bureau of Labor Statistics

the growth in total-factor productivity has been due to "the residual," a catchall term for technical change, which includes improvements in the quality of labor, management, and the equipment and techniques used in the production process.

Technical change provides virtually limitless ways of enhancing productivity. However, one cannot regard the inputs to productivity growth as falling into three discrete categories: labor, capital, and technological change. Rather, there is a synergistic relationship among improvements in each of these categories. Raising the quality of labor is essential to using advanced technology in much the same way that advanced technology empowers higher-skilled workers to perform at their peak. But without up-to-date physical plant and skilled management practices, technology and quality of labor will have little competitive impact.

Sound economic policy and organization can make a critical contribution to the growth process. Open markets and free exchange allocate human and physical resources to their best uses over the long-run. Industrial development leads to economies of scale and lower production costs, and profit incentives spur innovation. And macroeconomic stability provides an environment conducive to a long-term perspective in investment and other business decision making.

A competitive nation and the rising living standards it promises cannot be developed strictly by government mandate. Instead, it will require the active participation of business, the American citizenry, and the government. As a business-related organization, CED recognizes the vital role that the business community can play in this partnership and urges business to play a leading role in renewing America's ability to lead.

A. INVESTING IN PEOPLE

Rapid technological change over the past fifty years has fueled the integration of the world economy. Advances in transportation have accelerated the movement of people and products. New achievements in telecommunications and data processing have exponentially boosted the ability of workers to obtain, manipulate, and transmit information. Most significantly, new developments in manufacturing technology and process controls have transformed the way that products are made. Both the rate and the depth of these technological breakthroughs have revolutionized the world of work. The new workplace demands higher skills from entrants to the work force, and the dizzying rate of continuing technological change requires that workers be able to adapt quickly to new technologies.

The mere existence of a large and highly sophisticated capital stock will not boost productivity all by itself; its potential has to be unlocked by workers. The ability of the labor force to take advantage of the capital stock at its disposal is a critical link between investment and growth. A recent study by John Bishop of Cornell University has demonstrated the concrete link between academic achievement and productivity growth.[2]

In a world in which capital equipment, raw materials, and technology are flowing ever more freely, a country's productive edge will increasingly hinge on investments in human capital — those investments in education, training, and management skills that allow managers and workers to make the most of new technologies. The integration of the world economy means that global companies, whether headquartered in the United States, Japan, or Europe, have global alternatives and will take high-value-added work to where the highly-skilled workers are. Although the United States was once considered to be the home of the most skilled work force in the world, it is in real danger of losing this title.

The wages of lower-skilled U.S. workers are under strong downward pressure as a result of global economic integration, as illustrated by an 8 percent decline since 1974 in the real mean earnings of men who have only completed high school[3] (Figure 16). Unless the United States can increase the skill levels of all its workers, it will make little progress in narrowing the income gap between different segments of society.[4]

Although the scope and effect of some of the changes have been overstated in recent years, the gradual aging of our population will place a special premium on a more productive work force. Over the next decade, the rates of growth in the prime working-age population and the retirement population will be roughly equal. This parity is a significant change from the prior twelve years, when the average annual growth of the 25-to-54-year-old group was significantly higher than for those 55 and over. In the future, we will have relatively fewer working-age people than in the past to support a relatively larger and older retired population. This means that tomorrow's workers will need to be exceptionally productive.

Figure 16

Real Mean Earnings for Male High School Graduates
1975-1991

Thousands of 1990 Dollars

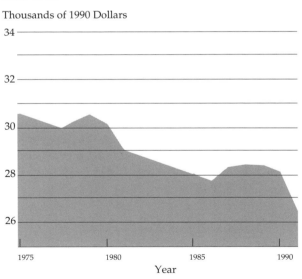

SOURCE: Current Population Reports, Series P-60 U.S. Bureau of the Census

The work force of the 1990s will also be more diverse. Labor force growth rates for blacks, Hispanics, and Asians will greatly exceed those for whites, and the growth rate for women will exceed that for men within all races.[5] Preparing this changing work force for the demands of work will require new approaches to the development of human potential that emphasize learning, flexibility, and productive participation in work and society throughout the entire life-cycle. America needs a new strategy for human investment — one that views human-resource development as a continuum from birth through retirement.

Investments in all our human capital will have another important effect on both our quality of life and our position in the community of nations. **The growing gap between rich and poor in this nation and the parallel implication that the United States is no longer the land of opportunity for all limit our ability to serve as a model for other countries and weaken our claim to be a rallier.** Expanding opportunity to all citizens will have profound economic benefits for America. In the global economy, the costs of poverty and a seemingly permanent underclass — reflected in the costs of health care, crime prevention, and welfare — are burdens our nation can no longer afford to bear.[6]

CREATING TOMORROW'S WORK FORCE

Concern over the quality of America's work force has led to a decade-long focus on what has been perceived as the failure of the public elementary and secondary schools to produce graduates adequately prepared for productive work. Perhaps no other domestic issue has so galvanized business leaders and policy makers at all levels of government. A recent Louis Harris study, sponsored by CED, dramatized the widening gap between the skills needed by today's workplace and the abilities possessed by new entrants to the work force. Only one employer in ten believed that recent high school students could solve complex problems.[7]

A decade of reform efforts at the state and local levels has produced little or no improve-

ment in student achievement. According to the most recent data from the National Assessment of Educational Progress, after a decade of steady decline through the 1970s, the achievement levels of American students in four core areas — math, science, reading, and civics — has improved only enough to bring students up to the levels achieved by their parents' generation in 1970 (Figure 17).

This situation is disturbing in its own right, but it also has very real implications for the future prosperity of our nation. Comparing our current performance with our past achievements has little relevance in a flexible global economy. Our students are preparing for participation in a world more technologically advanced than their parents could have imagined. Today's students should be expected to compete with the best in the world. Unfortunately, they cannot. On most international assessments of achievement in such critical subjects as science and mathematics, American students consistently rank well behind the United States' major economic competitors (Figures 18 and 19, pages 66 and 67).

Underlying the national reform movement is the widespread agreement that schools need to be substantially restructured to meet the demands of a more global, technology-based economy. There is also a growing appreciation of the role schools need to play in preparing young people for community life if our democratic institutions are to endure. By the beginning of the 1990s, CED developed a practical framework for national education reform, that emphasized the following principles:[8]

- Performance goals and standards for learning, and accountability for performance need to be specified on the national, state, and local levels.

- Greater flexibility in the use of resources and increased decision-making authority at the school level for teachers and principals and a greater role for parents.

- Community resources to meet the growing social and health needs of children and youths, particularly the disadvantaged, which are compromising their ability to learn.

- Improved training, recruitment, and performance incentives for qualified teachers.
- Equitable distribution of educational resources among wealthy and poor school districts.
- Introduction of market incentives within the public school system, as part of a total restructuring effort, which will help to spur institutional change and greater innovation and to provide more diverse learning opportunities.

- An increased focus on science and math as key areas for curriculum and pedagogical improvement.

EARLY INTERVENTION AND THE SOCIAL AGENDA

As serious as the deficiencies of public education are — and they are indeed critical — public schools cannot carry the entire blame for the fall off in work skills. Numerous other institutions, both public and private, have a

---

Figure 17

Trends in Average Educational Proficiency in the U.S.
In four subject areas

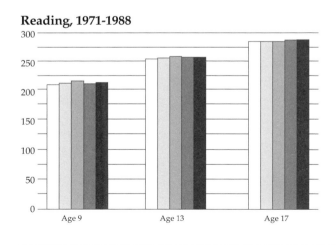

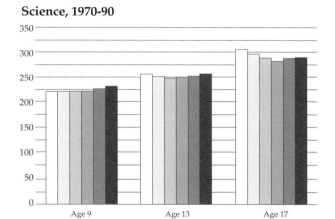

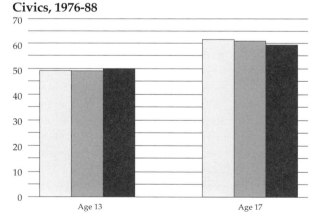

SOURCE: Educational Testing Service, National Science Board

NOTE: Math test years were 1973, 78, 82, 86, and 90. Science test years were 1970, 73, 77, 82, 86, and 90. Reading test years were 1971, 75, 80, 84, and 88. Civics test years were 1976, 82, and 88

critical impact on what young people learn, how well they learn, and how well they are prepared to assume adult roles in the workplace and in society. These include the family, the human services network, religious institutions, the health care system, employers, the media, and the community at large.

The last two decades have seen some astonishing changes in the demographic makeup of our population that lives in poverty. Although we have halved the percentage of the elderly in poverty since 1970,[9] our children have become the poorest group in society.[10] In the same period, the percentage of children under 18 in poverty has risen by more than 35 percent to its current level of 20.6 percent.

The high childhood poverty rate is of concern for a variety of reasons. (1) Children who are born into poverty generally receive poor prenatal or other preventive health care, rendering them susceptible to chronic health problems that can stunt proper development and cause a variety of learning disabilities. Of the 37 million U.S. citizens who have no health care coverage, 12 million are children. An estimated 12.5 percent of all children have suffered identifiable and preventable learning disabilities because of maternal drug use, smoking, or alcohol intake during pregnancy.[11] (2) Children who are raised in areas of concentrated poverty are likely to be exposed to a chaotic, often dangerous home and neighborhood environment. (3) Children whose poverty results from having parents who might be dropouts or poorly educated often fail to develop the critical language and learning skills in the first few years of life that are essential to later academic achievement. For these and other reasons, researchers at Teachers College, Columbia University, estimate that as many as 40 percent of all children are educationally disadvantaged in some way. In many urban centers, disadvantaged children are the majority.

Accordingly, CED has urged the nation to redefine education as a process that begins at

Figure 18

Average Science Scores for 13-Year-Olds
1991

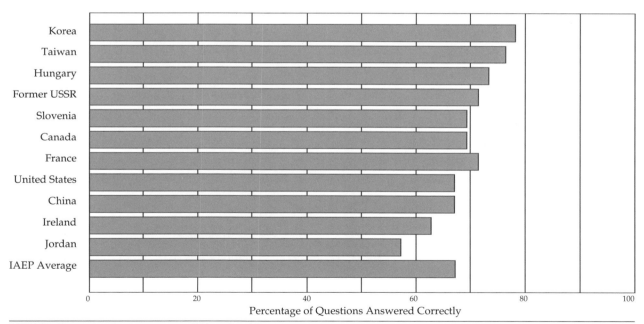

Percentage of Questions Answered Correctly

SOURCE: Center for the Assessment of Educational Progress

NOTE: All countries are representative of all students except for China, Canada, and the former USSR. China includes 20 of 29 provinces & independent cities, restricted grades, in-school population. Canada includes 9 of 10 provinces. The former USSR includes 14 of 15 Republics, Russian-speaking schools. IAEP Average includes more countries than listed in chart.

birth and includes the key components of child development: physical (including prenatal health), social, emotional, and cognitive. CED has also identified the growing social agenda (the matrix of social problems that inhibit children's ability to learn) that has been thrust upon schools by a rapidly changing society. Yet, few schools have either the human or financial resources, administrative flexibility, or institutional capacity to respond adequately to all the problems affecting children's health, development, and ability to learn. Early and sustained investment in the health and development of children can help to relieve schools of the social agenda and allow them to focus their resources on their traditional academic mission. The Head Start program is widely recognized as an effective way of investing in children before the start of school, and CED urges the federal government to expand its funding.

Other changes have also made it necessary for society to focus greater attention on the early development of all children. By 1988, well over half of all women with children under the age of 6 were in the work force. The Bureau of Labor Statistics estimates that by the year 2000, 47 percent of the work force will be female and that women will account for 62 percent of the net growth of the labor force between 1988 and 2000.[12] The composition of the "average" family is changing as well; between 1960 and 1990, the percentage of American children in single-parent households nearly tripled, from 9 percent to 24 percent. These effect of these trends is perhaps best illustrated by the doubling of the percentage of 3-to-5-year-olds that are in some form of preprimary school from 27 percent in 1965 to nearly 55 percent in 1989.[13]

The increasing number of mothers in the work force means that even very young children are spending more of their early development in some form of child care. A typical 3-year-old in full-time nonparental child care spends about half of his waking and learning

Figure 19

Average Math Scores for 13-Year Olds
1991

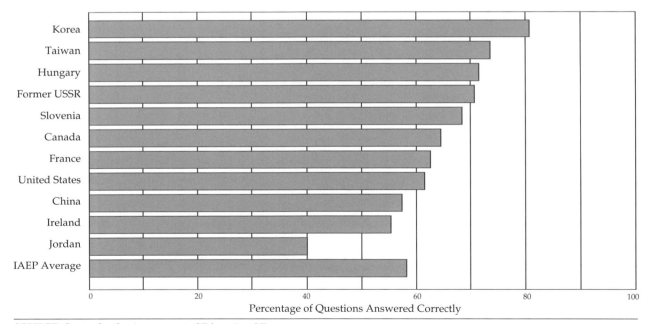

Percentage of Questions Answered Correctly

SOURCE: Center for the Assessment of Educational Progress

NOTE: All countries except China, Canada, and the former USSR are representative of all students. China included 20 of 29 provinces & independent cities, restricted grades, in school population. Canada includes 9 of 10 provinces. The former USSR includes 14 of 15 Republics, Russian-speaking schools. IAEP Average includes more countries than listed in chart.

hours in the care of adults other than his parents. The foundations of language proficiency and other key aspects of cognitive development, as well as critical social skills needed for later competency, are laid during the first five years of a child's life. **Therefore, the nation needs to improve the quality of children's early learning experiences, which increasingly are taking place under the auspices of child care**.

TRANSITION FROM SCHOOL TO THE WORKPLACE

Although fewer and fewer children are well prepared for the rigors of formal education, schools and employers seldom connect in ways that help young people make the transition from school to work. According to the National Center on Education and the Economy, "America may have the worst school-to-work transition system of any advanced industrial country. Students who know few adults to help them get their first job are left to sink or swim."[14] The average college student receives a combined public and private subsidy of $5,000 a year, but little is invested in the "forgotten half" of high school graduates who go directly into the work force. In the United States, fewer than one out of eight general education students enters a job with any occupation-specific vocational education preparation.[15]

A number of America's chief economic competitors, particularly Germany, do a better job of helping non-college-bound students make the transition to the work force by engaging them in apprenticeships that provide skill-specific training and real-world work experience. Although such programs have been criticized as politically impractical, they

---

EASING THE SCHOOL TO WORK TRANSITION

Our industrial competitors do a better job than the United States at helping non-college-bound students make the transition to the work force by providing them with apprenticeships that give students skill-specific training and real-world work experience. While these foreign models probably cannot be imported intact, they offer proof that business and education can work together productively to ease the transition into the work force. Studies also indicate that these programs, in addition to helping to build a substantive link between schools and the workplace, actually help boost the academic performance of students enrolled in them.[16]

American businesses are increasingly exploring such programs as a method of ensuring that they have a capable future work force. Although the mechanics of such programs vary, Sears Products Services has recently begun an initiative which utilizes the principles of foreign apprenticeship programs. The program, a partnership with local schools, combines on-the-job training and skill-specific classroom work with a general high school curriculum.

At the Davea Career Center near Chicago, students involved in the Sears program both learn how to repair Sears products and study the theory behind the products. Each student works at his/her own pace with a Sears in-house training instructor on hand to give assistance. Students are introduced to the company's products and learn many of the skills required to fix them. Students in the program also gain experience at a nearby Sears service center where they handle merchandise and mix with repair technicians. The technicians themselves have been trained to deal with teenagers and serve as mentors to the students.

The program lasts two years, the first year focusing on electrical training and the second year focusing either on advanced electronics or heating/air systems. Students spend nine hours a week "shadowing" their mentors and fifteen hours a week at the Career Center. Students also continue their standard education in order to learn non-technical aspects of their trade such as writing reports, conducting research on a computer, or interacting with customers.

Although there is no guarantee of employment with Sears, most students who have completed the program end up working for the company. The program is relatively small, but Sears hopes that its success can be replicated at many of its 750 service centers around the country.

offer proof that business and education can form a lasting and productive partnership.

We recommend the following approaches to improving the school-to-work transition:

- Vocational education programs should be redesigned so that they more effectively combine training in marketable skills with academic learning. One approach, based on foreign models, is for employers and schools to work together to create apprenticeship programs. Acquiring this type of practical experience should enable the graduate to compete successfully for a job. Thus far, the limited participation of American business has hampered the development of many successful domestic apprenticeship programs.

- Employers and schools should provide young people, especially those who expect to enter the work force directly after high school, with better incentives to work harder while in school. One strategy is for prospective employers to request high school transcripts or report cards. Businesses can also participate in programs that help students compile a portfolio of their achievements in academics and service. Schools need to encourage this process by making grade reports available to employers and presenting them in a standard format.

HEALTH AND U.S. HUMAN CAPITAL

Recently, public debate in the United States has focused on the issue of spiraling health care costs for the country as a whole. Despite their growing size, these escalating costs have failed to purchase world-class health care for our society. Yet, the health of American workers is vital to their performance. Accordingly, health care expenditures should be thought of as an investment in human capital, like education.

Since 1950, U.S. health care costs have consumed a larger and larger proportion of GDP. In 1950, we spent 4.4 percent of our GNP on health care; by 1970, we were spending 7.4 percent; and by 1990 the health sector was consuming more than 12 percent of GDP. Figure 20 shows that health care costs in other industrial countries, which also grew over the last few decades, have stabilized in recent years. As result of the faster and continued growth of our costs, the United States was devoting 12.4 percent of GDP to health care costs in 1990, whereas Japan, Germany, and Canada were devoting 6.5 percent, 8.1 percent, and 8.5 percent, respectively. At the current rate of growth, U.S. health care expenditures will rise to 15 percent to 17 percent of GDP by the year 2000.

These increases in health care expense would not be a problem if they were matched by rising levels of quality of care. Greater expenditures can contribute to a healthier, more productive work force, which would lead to productivity gains and economic growth.

Unfortunately, the current mix of expenditures does not maximize the health of America's human capital. Just as some of our citizens are receiving the best education in the world while others are denied access to a decent education, our health care system provides world-class care to some and inferior

Figure 20

National Health Expenditures
1960-90

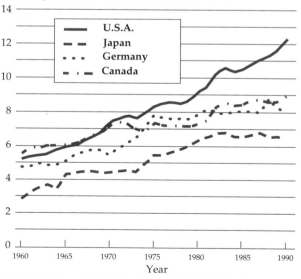

SOURCE: Organization for Economic Co-operation and Development

69

care for others. As many as 35 million Americans are currently uninsured, approximately 80 percent of them from working families. Moreover, many nonworking poor are denied access to public health insurance by arbitrary welfare rules; and scores of workers have inadequate insurance. The gaps in our health care system are illustrated by our comparatively high infant mortality rate and the relatively low life expectancy of our citizens (Table 4).

Achieving quality care for all our citizens at a cost that does not compromise the economic health of our country, needs to become a national objective. Because business is such a large consumer of insurance and other health services, and because it has a vital stake in both the health of the American work force and the cost of care, there is an important role for it to play in shaping health care reform in this country. CED urges market-oriented reform of both public and private health care systems, which will foster the competition needed to keep costs in line and quality high.

MANAGING HUMAN CAPITAL IN THE NEW WORLD ECONOMY

For American business to respond successfully to the wide array of changes facing it, new principles of management will need to be brought into play. In a fierce global market continually reshaped by relentless technological change, a well-educated work force and a high level of capital investment will be necessary but not sufficient for competitive success. **Fundamental changes in the way organizations are managed will be needed if American managers are to capture the benefits of higher-quality American labor.**

PEOPLE AND ORGANIZATION

For too long, some American firms have been captive to inflexible and hierarchical organizational structures. The hierarchical model is ill suited to the new global economy in several ways: Its lack of flexibility gives businesses little ability to adjust quickly to new processes, new products, and new technolo-

Table 4

1989 Health Indicators

	Life Expectancy at Birth		Infant Mortality (per 1000 live births)	Doctors Per 10,000 Population
	Male	Female		
Japan	75.9	81.8	4.6	16
Germany*	71.8	78.4	7.5	30
U.S.	71.5	78.5	9.7	23
U.K.	71.5	78.4	7.5	30
France	72.4	80.6	7.5	30
Canada*	73	79.8	7.2	22
Holland	73.7	80	6.8	24

*1988 and 1986 Data

SOURCE: U.S. Bureau of Labor Statistics

gies. Employees tend to feel little connection to quality. When work roles are too narrowly defined, there is not enough of the cross-fertilization that normally occurs when people switch positions or bring new perspectives to a process. Most important, management planning often fails to include the perspective of those who know the products, services, and their creation best: front line employees.

Reversing this situation will require the active participation of both labor unions and the workers themselves, but the chief responsibility for initiating the process lies with managers. American business needs to begin by communicating, in both language and policy, the interest that employees have in productive and competitive companies. A recent survey by the U.S. Chamber of Commerce found that only 9 percent of American workers believed that they would benefit from improvements in their firms' competitive position, while 93 percent of Japanese workers believed that their well-being was linked to their company's.[17] In the past few years, we have seen many remarkable examples of American companies successfully redesigning their organizations to enable them to compete more effectively, but many more have a long way to go.

The work environment needs to become less hierarchical, with fewer employee levels and a greater emphasis on cooperative effort. Employees should be encouraged to learn a wider variety of skills and to share their ideas with management. Production of goods and delivery of services should be redefined as collaborative efforts, partnerships between employees and their managers in which everyone benefits from a firm's competitive success. Workers should be rotated through a variety of positions and supported in their efforts to broaden their knowledge. By broadening the skill base of its employees and creating an ethic of flexibility and cooperation in the workplace, business can seize new technological opportunities and respond quickly to shifts in demand. As we mentioned earlier in this statement, government can play an important role in this process through changes in federal tax policy.

Neither management nor labor can now afford the adversarial relationships that have characterized American industrial organiza-tion. Formalized relationships between the two groups are an important method of fostering this type of partnership. Management needs to work with labor unions to eliminate work rules that inhibit flexibility. In return for their partnership, workers and unions should attain higher levels of employment security. Even apart from commitments to employment security on the part of their company, workers in a more flexible workplace will be assembling a portfolio of marketable skills.

At the same time, business should strategically restructure compensation practice, for both managers and workers, so that compensation more accurately reflects long-term performance. Paying for performance will require more effective goal setting and performance measurement. Structured channels for open discussion of ideas, evaluation of performance, and goal setting are critical components of strategic management in a new global economy.

The energy and entrepreneurship of America's people have long been our greatest competitive strengths. Unleashing creativity and enthusiasm through fundamental changes in the management practices will be a vital component of a competitive future. Without the flexibility and commitment to quality that newer management structures help foster, American business will not be able to adapt rapidly (and continuously) to the changes that are remaking the world economy.

TRAINING

The average American company currently spends about 1 percent of payroll on formal training, and only a few employers are devoting as much as 3 or 4 percent to this purpose. The high cost of formal training programs tends to restrict them to elite professional and technical workers. American business is failing to capture the potential gains in productivity and competitiveness that might be achieved by increasing investments in the education and training of workers. Employers should budget for education and training just as they do for investments in physical capital. But we realize that businesses are unlikely to realize the full social benefits of investments in training and that public subsidy is therefore appropriate. **CED supports changes in U.S.**

tax policies that could stimulate new investment in employee training and development. Federal support for training and new state policies to encourage individuals to invest in themselves might eventually recoup their costs in the form of taxes paid on increased individual and corporate earnings. However, given the large federal budget deficit, we believe that such tax credits should be financed through other revenue increases or budget reductions.

GLOBAL HORIZONS

To enjoy the full benefits of the truly global economy, American businesses and workers need to pursue opportunities on a global scale. Long blessed with a large and rapidly growing national economy and with abundant national resources, American business has traditionally had significant opportunities for growth within the nation's borders. Unfortunately, this has allowed many American businesses and members of government to ignore the rapidly globalizing world economy. Despite the global presence of some U.S. companies, the overwhelming majority of U.S. businesses have a strong domestic focus. According to the Productivity Policy Council, only 3 percent of American firms are active in more than five countries, and just 15 percent of American companies account for a substantial majority of our international economic activity.[18]

This myopia cannot persist if Americans want to enjoy a rising standard of living in future years. Both business executives and society in general need to adopt a global outlook. Businesses need to apply a longer-term perspective to building market share in foreign nations and tailoring products to meet differing national standards and tastes. Government needs to continue its efforts to open foreign markets to U.S. products and to support exporting to a level commensurate with our major industrial competitors through export credits, trade missions, and information about markets. Current government supports for exporting and international activity need to be retargeted toward small businesses, which are in greater need of government support.

DIRECTIONS FOR POLICY

1. People are America's greatest resource and the foundation of future U.S. economic strength. CED urges government, business, and community institutions to develop a comprehensive human investment strategy to ensure that our work force meet the needs of today's and tomorrow's workplace.

2. Any attempt to strengthen the quality of America's work force must begin with an early and sustained commitment to the health and development of our children. Government can expand Head Start to reach all children and ensure that care is available for pregnant women and their children. Business can help by developing innovative approaches to family policy, including child care, for its employees. Innovative family policies will not only help secure the future of the American work force but can also prove a powerful incentive for retaining quality workers.

3. National education reform is vital to America's economic future. Any reform strategy should place a high priority on the following: performance goals at the local and national levels; recruiting, retaining, and empowering good teachers; and equitable distribution of resources among districts with differing levels of wealth. Market incentives, which can be a useful means of improving educational quality, should be introduced in the public schools only as part of a comprehensive reform package. Experimentation with broader mechanisms, however, would be useful. Communities need to mobilize support for families and schools to ensure that children receive the support and encouragement they need throughout their educational careers.

4. U.S. business and government need to develop a national system for ensuring that students who do not plan to attend college learn applicable skills and receive training at the secondary level. Viable foreign models abound, and the United States should apply their lessons to our labor pool.

5. CED encourages increased federal support for business investment in human capital and state programs to encourage individuals to boost their own skill levels. Businesses should recognize the value of investing in human capital.

6. Quality health care is a critical part of our system of human investment. CED urges market-oriented reform of both public and private health systems, which will foster the competition needed to keep costs in line and quality high.

7. To make the best use of both labor and physical capital, and to allow business to adapt more readily to a continuously changing world economy, business and labor need to cooperate in redesigning the workplace. Leaner, more flexible organizations, where workers feel that they have a real stake in quality and performance, are best equipped for the realities of the new global economy.

B. INVESTING IN PHYSICAL CAPITAL AND INNOVATION

Second in importance only to the quality of our workers are the quantity and quality of "tools" that they use. A key element of sustained productivity growth is new investment in physical capital. Adding or improving capital equipment can enable workers to make more productive use of their time. Upgrading equipment can also result in improved production processes and economies of scale, allowing a company's output to increase while the number of employees remains constant. The impact of capital investment on productivity has been strongly supported by empirical evidence. Statistical analyses indicate that a 1 percent increase in the capital-labor ratio is associated with at least 0.33 percent of additional productivity growth, an exceedingly strong correlation.[19]

Another factor that plays a vital role in productivity growth is innovation. It affects the quality, composition, and application of the capital stock as new investment in physical capital allows the economy to translate scientific advance into commercial application. Innovation has long been a strength of the U.S. economy. Before World War II, the United States experienced three great periods of innovation, each of which lasted about half a century. The first, based on cotton textiles, iron, and steam power, lasted from the end of the American Revolution until the 1840s. The second push, based on the building of the railroads, and on steel, lasted until the 1890s. The third, powered by electricity and the automobile, carried the United States through the first half of the twentieth century.

It is harder to fasten a label on the fourth period of innovation that got under way during World War II because it was based, not on any one or two innovations, but on a flood of them stemming from what may be called the *research revolution*. The wartime and postwar innovations owe their origin to scientific progress in nuclear and solid-state physics, organic and inorganic chemistry, electronics, engineering, mathematics, computer science, the earth sciences, the biological sciences.

The United States has invested heavily in such advances and has scored many successes. But, as Frank Press, President of the National Academy of Science, has observed: "To the consternation of many inventors, such products as fiber optics, carbon-fiber reinforced plastics, monoclonal antibodies, integrated circuits, jet engines, magnetic recording, and office copying machines all have one thing in common — they were conceived in one country, yet other countries led in their commercialization."[20]

Recent reports indicate that the U.S. problems in innovation extend beyond the ability to commercialize discoveries. In some areas, the United States has fallen behind in the ability to generate the discoveries themselves. In a recent *Business Week* ranking of the most innovative corporations, companies headquartered in Japan occupied the top four slots.[21]

The decline in U.S. innovation and our decreasing ability to capitalize on new ideas are partly attributable to a disturbing trend over the past thirty years: The United States has consistently invested less than its major economic competitors. This trend is seen in the decreasing amount of resources devoted to net capital formation. Between 1960 and 1990, our expenditures on net capital formation, expressed as a percentage of GDP, declined from 8.0 percent to 3.8 percent, a 52 percent drop. Although there were declines in all the major industrialized countries, the U.S. decline was the most dramatic (Figure 21). Moreover, in 1990, Germany's rate of net capital formation was two and a half times America's, and Japan's was practically five times America's.

A national goal in the coming decade and century must be to make a more concerted effort to increase investment in our future and to do a better job of gaining the economic benefits of our scientific and technological breakthroughs. This will require that government, business, and universities work together to strengthen our productivity and facilitate the commercialization of our advances in science and technology.

Figure 21

Net Capital Formation
1960-1990

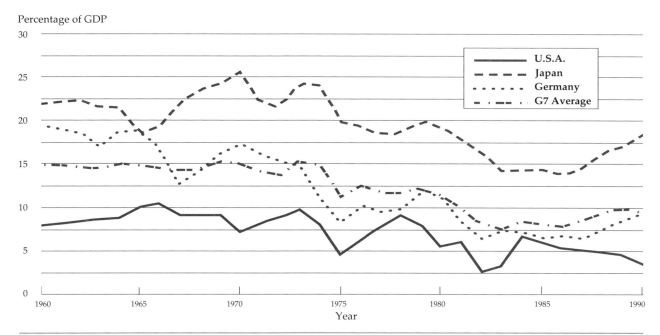

Percentage of GDP

SOURCE: Organization for Economic Co-operation and Development

NOTE: 1961 data not available

TECHNOLOGY IN THE GLOBAL ECONOMY

Technological advances will do much to determine America's role in the evolving global economy. Creating a pattern of constant innovation and capturing the benefits of this innovation will be essential to maintaining and improving the nation's living standards in the years ahead. Technological innovation is central to any strategy for U.S. economic competitiveness because it enables workers to be more productive. At the same time, workers who have better skills can more readily embrace rapid and continuing changes in technology or process. Increasing the skills of the work force and strengthening the culture of innovation in society can work to mutually reinforce one another.

The changing composition of the American economy has been a source of much recent debate. Over the past twenty years, the share of America's labor force employed by the manufacturing sector has steadily declined, causing concern among those who argue that the manufacturing sector, vital to our economic health, is in irreversible decline. In fact, the opposite is true. The percentage of workers employed in manufacturing fell because manufacturing firms were trimming excess capacity and becoming more productive. With this improvement in productivity, manufacturing's share of real GDP has remained roughly constant over the past twenty years.

Those who suggest that manufacturing is somehow more important to the economy than the services sector recognize the benefits of a strong manufacturing base, but they fail to acknowledge that services add similar value in the market. Since, by some definitions, services employ more than 80 percent of the American work force, productivity increases in this sector are most critical to rising living standards. A robust services sector — producing health care, finance, engineering, computer software, law, and entertainment — is a vital component of our national economy. In addition to elevating our standard of living, such services have been among the most globally competitive American ventures.

THE AMERICAN WAY IN TECHNOLOGY: WAR AND PEACE

The payoffs from organized research in World War II helped convince both the public and American industry of the benefits of government and business cooperation in technology. The Office of Scientific Research and Development (OSRD) initiated many of the technological advances that helped to win the war. Most dramatic was the Manhattan Project, which enlisted and coordinated the talents of many specialists in the urgent quest for the atomic bomb. Similarly, in the chemical industry, a search was organized to find ways to replace natural rubber, supplies of which were threatened by the sea war. In these and other achievements such as radar, antibiotics, and perhaps most important of all, computers, one can find ample support for the thesis that wartime research powered the greatest technological breakthroughs of the twentieth century.

The problem is whether such a pattern for success can be carried over from wartime to peacetime research and development. For the United States, it is an old and vexing problem. In November 1944, with the end of the war in sight, President Roosevelt wrote to Vannevar Bush, the distinguished engineer who headed OSRD, to ask his advice on four fundamental questions: (1) What could be done, consistent with military security, to make known to the world, as soon as possible, the contributions made during the war effort to science and technology? (2) What could be done to organize a program for continuing the research, spurred by the war, in medicine and related sciences? (3) What could the government do to aid research activities by public and private organizations and to deal with the interrelation between them? (4) Could an effective program be proposed for discovering and developing scientific talent in American youth, to assure the future of scientific research in this country? "The diffusion of such knowledge," said Roosevelt, "should help us stimulate new enterprises, provide jobs for our returning servicemen and other workers, and make possible great strides for the improvement of the national well-being."

Ironically, because the end of World War II gave way to the beginning of the Cold War, we have been able to defer answering some of these questions for the past fifty years, as we continued to invest in military technology and research. Since 1970, the United States has continued to outpace its closest industrial competitors in total resources devoted to research and development, but its lead in R&D expenditures as a percentage of GDP has evaporated when compared with those of Japan and Germany (Figures 22).

These trends are potentially more damaging than they appear. The United States has directed a much higher percentage of its research spending to defense-related R&D than any of its competitors have (Figure 23). Although these expenditures have had a significant number of commercial applications, they have not enhanced productivity in the same way that nondefense research expenditures would have.

INNOVATION, GROWTH, AND THE U.S. GOVERNMENT

The success of U.S. industries in the global economy illustrates that private businesses, engaged in direct competition with one another, can be sources of powerful new ideas. Despite the success of private enterprise acting alone, **there are several ways in which the federal government can (and in many places already does) play an important role in the development, application, and diffusion of new technology.**

Government can cultivate an environment that encourages business to develop and apply new ideas. James S. Langer, of the Institute for Theoretical Physics of the University of California, observes that "it is not just lack of vision or pig-headedness that causes American manufacturing industries to resist introducing new materials or advanced processes." Rather, "the cost of introducing new technologies in this country is enormous; capital is expensive, licensing can be risky and time consuming and, if the product is really novel, the

Figure 22

Total Research and Development Expenditures
1962-89

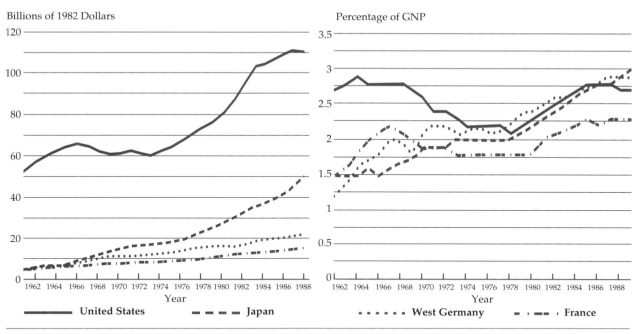

Billions of 1982 Dollars

Percentage of GNP

SOURCE: National Science Board

Figure 23

Non-Defense Research and Development Expenditures
1971-89

Percentage of GNP

SOURCE: National Science Board

materials manufacturer is exposed to a variety of legal hazards."[22]

The relationship among industry, government, and science — and between research and economic growth — is extremely complex. Big spending on research has led to rapid development of many fields — and to big profits for some organizations. But the quest for profits and grants may hurt science itself, and thereby choke off long-term economic growth.

A study by the National Academy of Engineering declares: "The highest priority for strengthening the technical foundations and thereby the long-term wealth-generating capacity of the U.S. economy must be to make the United States a more attractive place for individuals, companies, and other institutional entities, regardless of national origin, to conduct the full complement of technical activities critical to the nation's long-term prosperity and security."[23] In addition to developing a high-quality work force, there are a number of ways in which our nation can achieve this objective.

Reducing the Cost of Capital. The problem of lagging American investment in materials, equipment, and research has macroeconomic roots. The low national saving rate and chronic federal budget deficits raise the cost of capital for individual concerns and curb capital formation for the nation as a whole, permitting competitors in other countries to take the lead. Nothing has a greater effect on the ability of the United States to innovate and to profit from innovation than the macroeconomic environment. Cutting the budget deficit and lifting the rate of national saving will free resources for productive investment. The resulting lower interest rates would enable businesses to make patient investments in research and in the physical capital needed to convert research into marketable products.

The federal government can also provide tax incentives for businesses to invest in innovation or physical plant and equipment and remove unproductive tax subsidies. **The government should make the tax credit for research and development permanent and provide more equal treatment for productivity-enhancing business investment, as compared with residential housing, in the tax code.**

Direct Research. Contrary to public perception, the federal government has actively supported innovation and scientific advancement. Although much of this research was undertaken to meet security needs, even defense-related research has generated substantial commercial benefits. And despite an overall focus on defense, federal funding for research, administered through such divergent channels as the Department of Agriculture, the National Institutes of Health, the Department of Energy, and the National Science Foundation, has resulted in a range of discoveries which have generated commercial applications and have benefited society as a whole. The end of the cold war and the corresponding cuts in military spending have engendered new debate about the government's role in developing new technology.

The end of the cold war offers the United States a unique opportunity to adjust its research priorities. **The federal government should not cut aggregate direct funding of research. Rather, it should begin to shift resources to financing the development of technologies for civilian use.** This shift may require changing the mission of federal research agencies. Even as the federal government seeks to cut defense-related expenditures, it needs to recognize that basic or generic research (advanced research whose benefits span industries and companies) should not be left entirely to the private sector. Because the risks of this type of investment are so high and significant rewards often accrue to society as a whole rather than to one specific company, the private sector is likely to underfund basic research. Small federal investments in this type of research can also help convene industry-wide consortiums in which individual firms share the risk and work to disseminate new technology.*

One vital but often-overlooked competitive resource is the U.S. system of federal laboratories. These giant research facilities have spawned some of the most remarkable technologies of our time, many of which were initially intended for military use but proved to be commercial breakthroughs as well. Unless their formidable talents and resources are redirected toward commercial use, these facilities will fall victim to declining military budgets. (At Los Alamos, perhaps the most renowned of these labs, 75 percent of the work is still defense-related.) As the funding for military projects declines, the intellectual firepower of these labs needs to be trained on other critical problems: the environment, medical technology, energy needs, advanced communications, and manufacturing technology. The labs also should be encouraged and enabled to continue to work with private companies and industry consortia, as directed by the 1989 Cooperative Research and Development Agreement. Business also needs to take a more active role in pursuing joint arrangements with these labs.

Dissemination of technology: The failure of American companies to capture benefits of American discoveries can be partly blamed on

---

*See memoranda by ELMER B. STAATS, (page 89).

78

the high cost of capital, but the United States also needs to become more effective in the dissemination of technological advances.

One important step that can be taken to encourage rapid commercial application of research gains and coherent application of federal research funds would be for one central office, perhaps the President's Office for Science and Technology Policy, to coordinate and monitor all federally funded research.[24] A special priority needs to be given to disseminating process technology: part of the reason the reason that the United States seems to have trouble converting innovation into economic growth is that effective processes (the means of turning technological breakthroughs into commercial successes) are not in wide use. At the same time, the federal government could support the efforts of thriving state and regional technology centers, which share scientific advances with local industry, by providing federal matching funds.[25]

We can also help speed dissemination of new technology by maintaining and expanding the data networks and computer systems that bind our research facilities and universities together. The request by the President's Assistant for Science and Technology, D. Allen Bromley, for money to upgrade Internet (a national set of computer networks) into a National Research and Education Network is an excellent start. The government can also play a critical role in setting standards that allow new technologies to be shared and replicated.

Protectionism can be as dangerous to a nation in the realm of science and technology as it is in trade. The pool of scientific and technological knowledge is global, and we must draw from it as well as contribute to it, if we are to maintain our place of leadership in the world economy. This means not only a free international flow of scientific papers and researchers but also welcoming foreign investment in our own country, as our businesses want to be welcomed abroad. **Accordingly, CED recommends that any government incentives for conducting research be extended to foreign firms engaged in research here, assuming, of course, that similar incentives are available on a reciprocal basis to U.S. firms abroad.**

Higher Education. America's universities are already one of the crown jewels of our nation's competitive position, but here, too, research stands to suffer if federal cutbacks in defense curtail the amount of support for research. Of the Defense Department's funding for basic research, 57 percent goes to colleges and universities. Much of this supports vital work in engineering. **Because our nation cannot afford to let the quality of its university research facilities erode, we need to ensure that if defense funds are trimmed they are replaced by direct support for research.** Although recent disagreements about the appropriation of government funds by universities have called the effectiveness of these programs into question, cutting funding for university research is the wrong response. Tighter controls may be needed, but the vast majority of federal support for university research is money well spent.

Our universities also need to adapt their practices to the demands of a new global marketplace. They need to engage in a constructive partnership with secondary school educators that will encourage young people, especially minorities and women, to pursue careers in science. Universities also need to stress team-oriented research methods which more closely emulate the way research is carried out in industry. Lastly, universities should recognize that the ability to share research or engage in joint enterprises with scientists from other countries is vital to the advancement of scientific knowledge. Accordingly, they should encourage study of foreign languages and cultures as part of any curriculum, even the sciences.[26]

Regulation. Debate over the role of the government in helping American industry has too often been dominated by those arguing for or against aggressive government intervention to bolster an industry. An important role for government that is often ignored in disagreements over industrial policy is to ensure that regulations do not unnecessarily handicap American industry. Careful review and rationalization of government regulations or barriers affecting American business is more permanent in its effects, more in accord with market forces, and less prone to government miscalculations than any direct intervention.

Domestic regulation threatens our competitive position when businesses located elsewhere can operate without incurring the same regulatory costs as domestic producers. Many legal rules or government regulations constrain the ability of American business to compete internationally. Some of these constraints are intentional, but many are unintended side effects of measures aimed at other objectives. Provisions ranging from taxes to safety measures and from environmental rules to monopoly restraints have had such effects. Certainly, many of these rules have beneficial effects as well; and in some cases, the net social good is worth a slight effect on America's competitive position. But all too often, the regulations fail to achieve the social good or achieve it in an unnecessarily inefficient way. In an era of fierce global competition, we need to be especially vigilant in reevaluating rules and regulations that hamper the ability of American business to compete effectively in the global market.

Governments at all levels — federal, state, and local — also need to streamline and rationalize the regulatory process. Currently, regulations are imposed on business from a variety of directions and at an array of levels. When interviewing businesses about the regulatory obstacles that they faced, the MIT Commission on Industrial Productivity found that "a common complaint is that American firms are burdened by overlapping regulatory jurisdictions, complex and lengthy procedural requirements, and excessively detailed, prescriptive regulations promulgated by inflexible regulatory institutions."[28] In order to ensure that regulations are coherent, and do not unnecessarily constrain the ability of American business to continue creating jobs, a more cooperative partnership among business, government, labor, and the community will be required to root out inefficiency in regulation.

THE ROLE OF BUSINESS: TIME HORIZONS AND ONGOING INNOVATION

Not all the blame for low U.S. investment in capital and technology can be placed on

---

INFRASTRUCTURE

A growing body of scholarship asserts that governments have underinvested in infrastructure such as roads, bridges, and airports, in recent years. The proponents of more aggressive investments in infrastructure argue that as much as 60 percent of the slump in productivity growth is due to the "neglect of our core infrastructure."[27]

Closer analysis reveals that some areas have significant problems, but these problems tend to be specific to a few geographical locales. A recent study by the Office of Technology Assessment (OTA) found the costs of highway congestion to be $30 billion annually. OTA determined that more than two thirds of the cost is concentrated in six metropolitan areas. A study of highway pavement quality also found that more than two thirds of all miles in need of immediate repair are concentrated in 13 states. Rather than spreading

infrastructure investment evenly among states and municipalities, federal funding should be targeted to those areas where the payoff in productivity growth is highest. Such federal spending decisions are best determined by real economic need, and not by political pressure.

In addition to being misdirected by politics, public investments are seldom financed in ways that encourage efficient investment decisions and are often subjected to uneconomic and inappropriate use. After construction, the low cost of usage encourages overconsumption. Federal grants in support of infrastructure investments should be adjusted to give state and local authorities incentives for rational investment decisions. Pricing mechanisms which insure that public investment is appropriately related to economic costs — such as user fees — should also be more widely used.

government policy. Some of the blame has rightfully been directed at American executives. American businesses have often been criticized for pursuing excessive short-term profits and neglecting to make investments or other strategic decisions whose payoff may not be immediately apparent. Even American executives concede that their time horizons are noticeably shorter than those of their competitors in Japan and Europe. In a recent survey conducted by James Poterba of the Massachusetts Institute of Technology and Lawrence Summers of Harvard University and the World Bank for the Council on Competitiveness, only 6 percent of the Chief Executive Officers who responded believed that their time horizons were longer than their Asian competitors'; only 21 percent believed that their horizons were longer than their European competitors.[29]

This tendency can manifest itself in a variety of ways: failure to invest sufficient resources in research and development, neglect of physical capital, or an unwillingness to weather small margins in markets that will prove extremely lucrative in the future. Measured by two key indicators — business investment in physical capital and industry-funded research and development — American business as a whole has invested considerably less in the future than the business sectors in our major industrial competitors.[30]

At the same time, we should not make the mistake of assuming that this short-term outlook is an irrational response unique to American business. Our low rate of personal saving and large and seemingly intractable federal budget deficits suggest that this tendency to neglect the future is a societal phenomenon to which business reacts in the market. Our low national saving rate and the resulting high cost of capital discourage long-term investments. The cost of capital for American firms is also more volatile, making it extremely difficult to gauge the worth of an investment. A complex of shifting regulatory jurisdictions makes it extremely difficult to ascertain future constraints on business operations. Finally, the way in which American firms are financed, with much of their

stock sold on the open market, often to large institutional investors, significantly affects planning horizons. In Europe and Japan, large investors hold seats on boards and are in close contact with management, but the holders of American equity have no long-term loyalty to the corporations they own. Accordingly, corporate executives feel that this arrangement discounts or undervalues the worth of their organizations and forces them to focus more exclusively on short- term goals.[31]

We have already discussed some of the solutions to this problem: a permanent R&D tax credit, more rational regulation of industry, and a stable, growth-oriented macroeconomic policy that will lower the long-term cost of capital. We also need to rethink tax policies that are biased against productive investment. But these steps alone will not be enough. Business executives and society in general need to lengthen their time horizons. American industries that have consistently focused on the long term (such as the pharmaceuticals industry) have reaped substantial benefits and rank among the most globally competitive of American businesses.

DIRECTIONS FOR POLICY

1. It is essential that the U.S. government create an environment in which investment in human capital, physical capital, and technology will flourish. Budget policies need to stop fueling consumption and to encourage the growth of saving and investment. The federal budget should ultimately be brought to a modest surplus, lest chronic deficits undermine national saving and reduce the capital available for productive investment.

2. Changes in the federal tax system are needed to encourage long-term investment. These should include a permanent tax credit for investment in research and development. Tax provisions should be modified so that investments in housing are no longer heavily subsidized compared with productivity-enhancing business investments.

3. The United States is committed to free enterprise and competition as its basic pattern of industrial organization; this has served the nation well in both the discovery and the diffusion of technology. But our system has always provided an important role for government and academic institutions to play in promoting research and technological development. However, in the post cold war economy, direct federal support of science and technology needs to be reordered. Three-fourths of government expenditures on research and development have been devoted to military purposes. With declining military budgets ahead, government funding of research should shift toward the support of basic research in civilian technologies. The federal government should ensure that there is no net loss in federal funding for direct research because of cuts in defense expenditures.

4. Antitrust rules and other government regulations should be reviewed to insure that they do not unnecessarily constrain the ability of American business to compete in global markets. Government at all levels needs to be especially vigilant in ensuring that antitrust regulations do not prohibit businesses from engaging in cooperative research efforts.

5. American business also needs to recognize the benefits of patient investment in technology and research and development. Business leaders should note that the longer time horizons of their international competitors give foreign companies an advantage in a technology-driven global economy.

CHAPTER 5

CONCLUSION: A CALL TO ACTION

After World War II, the United States demonstrated that it could deal with long-range problems with more patience and consistency of purpose than its opponents or friends — or even its own leaders — had expected. Remembering the world's experience after World War I, when the United States had rapidly withdrawn its forces from Europe, had refused to join the League of Nations, and had retreated into isolationism, few could foresee that America would provide the leadership for the creation of the United Nations, the Marshall Plan, the North Atlantic Treaty Organization, and other long-lasting programs to rebuild the world's shattered economy and check the spread of communism in areas far from the United States. But all this happened and was carried through persistently over four decades, ultimately to stunning success. Furthermore, America accomplished its own transformation from a nation at war to one enjoying relative peace without the feared resurgence of the great depression. It launched an astonishing surge of broadly-based economic growth at home as well as abroad.

Yet, as so often has happened before, success in solving the problems of one era brings with it new challenges and hazards. Today, hard on the heels of the collapse of the Communist threat and the emergence of a single world economy dominated by the market democracies, there are new threats that must be overcome: Threats of economic collapse in the states of the old Soviet empire, conflicts among them, and risks that new dictatorships could arise; threats to the increasingly integrated world economy that would result from a new economic cold war among the capitalist powers; and the risk that the dangerous levels of poverty in the developing countries will worsen as their populations increase.

Those threats can be defeated only by the cooperative efforts of many nations. In bringing those cooperative efforts into effective action, we believe that the United States has a crucial role to play, as it did after World War II. But our role in the years ahead must be different from what it was when the United States was overwhelmingly the richest and most powerful country in the world.

We have conceived of America's new role as that of a rallier of nations. Our aim must be to work with and through other nations. If there is to be burden sharing, there must be power sharing as well. Adapting to this new role will not be easy: U.S. policymakers must be ready to completely overhaul the American role in world affairs and our foreign partners will need to do the same. As a rallier of nations, the United States needs to encourage other industrial nations to broaden their own perspectives and step up their commitments to addressing global issues. But this sharing of responsibilities and power should itself be a source of strength for world security and prosperity. The countries emerging from dictatorship and backwardness are looking to us to play that rallying role.

The Committee for Economic Development wholeheartedly rejects any suggestion that the United States can no longer afford to be a leader of nations. America has global responsibilities in accord with its global interests. Our nation's position of international leadership reflects our concern for the security of our own citizens and people worldwide, and our recognition that a global marketplace for goods, services, and ideas benefits citizens of all nations, especially our own.

Expanding economic links between nations and confronting a new array of challenges, ranging from the global environment to international security, will require new cooperation among nations. With our remarkable wealth and power and our commitment to democratic ideals, the United States is uniquely positioned to lead the development of these cooperative efforts. Although we can no longer go it alone, we should no longer want to. We have capable friends and allies throughout the world, most notably in Japan and Europe. They have skills and resources that can complement ours, and they share many of the same objectives. We call on them to join the United States in crafting an age of cooperation among nations based on mutual long-term interests and values that will replace the cold war relationships based on fear. This new pattern for international cooperation will require a change not only in U.S. thinking, but changes in the roles of our international partners: the United States must rally them to assume new roles in the conduct of world affairs.

And we call on the American citizenry to recognize that we live in a time of opportunity at home as well as abroad. Change seems to beget fear, but the changes that we have witnessed over the past years should remind the American people that we are a strong and resourceful nation capable of achieving both our international and domestic objectives on a grand scale. The new challenges abroad and those problems at home that have eroded our ability to lead are not insuperable. Moreover, in today's global economy, we can no longer look upon domestic and international challenges as issues for separate consideration. The opportunities created by export markets and by infusions of foreign capital and ideas are critical to an increasing American standard of living. At the same time, we must also address neglected problems at home that have weakened our capacity to lead.

Despite the complexity of the problems facing our world, our objectives as a rallier of nations can be reduced to the few key principles that we outlined in the beginning of the statement: An unwavering commitment to open markets and economic integration; cooperative efforts to ensure not only military security but a healthy global environment; and a renewed commitment to fostering sustainable economic growth in the developing world.

To play this leadership role effectively, the United States needs to achieve several domestic objectives as well. Reducing the mammoth federal budget deficit before it becomes an unfair burden on our children is the first step to renewing America's competitive potential. Our people have long been the foundation of the world's most productive economy; we need a comprehensive human investment strategy which strives to get *all* Americans ready for an increasingly complex workplace. Finally, the federal government needs to create an environment that encourages the innovation and excellence vital to our continued prosperity.

We believe these principles can add up to a comprehensive strategy that will enable the United States to stand in the forefront of needed global change for many years to come. In the new era that is beginning, America can achieve as much as it did in the exciting and in many ways astonishing era that is now ending.

Just as confronting new international problems will require a new spirit of cooperation among nations, invigorating our domestic economy and expanding its promise to all our citizens will require new partnerships at home. All segments of society — business, government, labor, the community — will need to play an active role if we are to move forward.

This strategy must be translated into action. Becoming a rallier of nations will require changing not only our thinking but our priorities. We need to transform institutions and governance structures — from local levels to the supranational — to achieve our strategy. We must also make hard choices. Only by reordering priorities can we free resources to carry out our goals. We call upon the President and Congress, on an urgent basis, to start working together to achieve the laws and initiatives and to provide the resources, human and financial needed to forge an effective and coherent global economic strategy for the United States and to assure its implementation. We call on international institutions and our partners in other nations to help construct new cooperative efforts designed for a new world. Finally, we call on our colleagues in the business, academic, and civic communities in the United States and around the world to play an active and constructive role in the process.

ENDNOTES

CHAPTER TWO

1. Patricia Ruggles and Charles F. Stone, "Income Distribution over the Business Cycle: Were the 1980's Different?," Prepared for the Annual Meeting of The Association for Public Policy and Management, 1991.

2. Competitiveness Policy Council, *Building a Competitive America: First Annual Report to the President & Congress*, (Washington: Competitiveness Policy Council, 1992), p. 14.

3. See Robert Z. Lawrence, "Emerging Regional Arrangements: Building Blocks or Stumbling Blocks," *American Express Bank Review*, 1991.

4. Ruggles and Stone

5. From a speech by Secretary of State James Baker 3rd, "America and the Collapse of the Soviet Empire: What Has to Be Done," on December 12, 1991 at Princeton University.

6. Joseph S. Nye, Jr., Kurt Biedenkopf, and Motoo Shiina, *Global Cooperation After the Cold War*, (New York: The Trilateral Commission 5, 1991); Steven Krasner, *Global Communications and National Power*, World Politics, April 1991, pp. 336-366.

7. Nye, Jr., Biedenkopf, and Shiina.

8. Ibid.

9. Joseph S. Nye, Jr., *Bound to Lead: The Changing Structure of American Power* (New York: Basic Books, 1990) pp. 73-77.

CHAPTER THREE

1. This section draws on a working paper written by Isaiah Frank entitled, "Some Notes for the Global Economic Strategy Project." Parts of Professor Frank's paper have been published as an article in *International Economic Insights* (Washington: Institute for International Economics, July-August 1991) under the title, "After the Uruguay Round."

2. Paul Krugman, "Is Free Trade Passe?" in *International Economics and International Economic Policy: A Reader*, Philip King ed., (New York: McGraw Hill Publishing Company, 1990) pp. 91-107.

3. Research and Policy Committee of the Committee for Economic Development, *An America That Works* (New York: Committee for Economic Development, 1990) pp. 92-94.

4. Research and Policy Committee of the Committee for Economic Development, *Breaking New Ground in U.S. Trade Policy*, (Boulder, Colorado: Westview Press, 1991) pp. 73-74.

5. U.S. Congress, Office of Technology Assessment, *Trade and the Environment: Conflict & Opportunities*, OTA-BP-ITE-94 (Washington, D.C: U.S. Government Printing Office, May 1992).

6. The GATT encompasses a very high proportion of the planet's countries. It currently has 108 member countries that are participating in the negotiations of the Uruguay Round and there are 29 other countries that have applied as de facto members. These de facto members have made a commitment to abide by whatever agreement is reached.

7. The Administration's strategy for dealing with environmental concerns in connection with NAFTA is set out in *Response of the Administration to Issues Raised in Connection with the Negotiation of a North American Free Trade Agreement*, transmitted by the President to Congress on May 1, 1991.

8. *Breaking New Ground in U.S. Trade Policy*, p. 12.

9. C. Fred Bergsten, "Commentary: The Move Toward Free Trade Zones," *Economic Review of the Federal Reserve Bank of Kansas City*, November/December 1991, p. 29.

10. Paul Krugman, "The Move Toward Free Trade Zones," *The Federal Reserve Bank of Kansas City Economic Review*, November/December 1991, p. 13.

11. Rosabeth Moss Kanter, "Transcending Business Boundaries: World Managers View Change" *Harvard Business Review*, May/June 1991, p. 151.

12. A recent study of 18 OECD countries found that in the period from 1989 to 1992, fourteen of the countries saw their structural budget deficits increase. See *OECD Letter*, August/September, 1992, p. 3.

13. In December 1992, CED will release a policy statement, *The Federal Budget and Economic Growth*, that will elaborate on these issues.

14. This does no mean that domestic spending should not be increased for *proven* productive public investment. CED has strongly supported increased expenditures for education, training, and certain public infrastructure. However these expenditures, which are properly considered increases in national savings and investment should be financed insofar as possible from reductions in related expenditures.

15. Research and Policy Committee of the Committee for Economic Development, *The Economy and National Defense: Adjusting to Military Cutback in the Post-Cold War Era*, (New York: CED, 1991).

16. U.S. Congress, Office of Technology Assessment, *After the Cold War: Living With Lower Defense Spending* (Washington: U.S. Government Printing Office, February 1991) p. 77.

17. Judith N. Shapiro, "From Mass to Lean Production: A Revolution in Business Ethics", *The World and I*, August 1992

18. CED, Research and Policy Committee of the Committee for Economic Development, *Battling America's Budget Deficits*, (New York: CED, 1989) p. 11.

19. See *The Economy and National Defense* and the forthcoming *Federal Budget and Economic Growth* (CED) for policy on using consumption resources for economic growth and the economic policies required.

20. Robert Solomon, "Background Paper" in *Partners in Prosperity: The Report of the Twentieth Century Fund Task Force on the Internation Coordination of National Economic Policies*, (New York: Priority Press Publications, 1991) pp. 96

21. The Bonn Summit of 1978 was the only negotiated fiscal and monetary package. The Plaza (1985) and Louvre (1987) agreements produced major coordinated exchange rate interventions designed to depreciate, and then stabilize, the dollar, but the underlying fiscal imbalances were addressed only in the communiques, not in major policy changes.

22. Richard N. Cooper, "Economic Interdependence and Coordination of Economic Policies," *Handbook of International Economics*, Vol. 2, (New York: North-Holland, 1985) pp. 1229 ff.

23. This chapter draws heavily on an earlier CED policy statement, *Finance and Third World Economic Growth* (Boulder, Colorado: Westview Press, 1988).

24. Statement by William H. Draper III at the National Press Club in Washington, D.C., April 23, 1992, pp. 3-4.

25. Donald H. May, *America's Stake in the Developing World*, (Washington, D.C.: The Citizen's Network for Foreign Affairs, 1990) p. 8.

26. Richard Feinberg and Peter Hakim, "Look Southward, US," *Christian Science Monitor*, January 15, 1992.

27. John W. Sewell and Stuart K. Tucker, eds., *Growth, Exports and Jobs in a Changing World Economy: Agenda 1988*, (Washington, D.C.: Overseas Development Council, 1988) pp. 10-16.

28. John W. Sewell, Peter M. Storm, and Contributors, *Challenges and Priorities in the 1990's*, (Washington, D.C.: Overseas Development Council, 1992) p. 16.

29. May, p. 5.

30. The World Bank, *World Development Report 1992* (New York: Oxford University Press, 1992).

31. The World Bank, *World Development Report 1990* (New York: Oxford University Press, 1990) p. 10.

32. Speech by Lawrence Summers before the NIIA in Lagos, Nigeria, "The Challenges of Development," November 8, 1991, p. 3.

33. The United Nations Development Programme, *Human Development Report 1992*, (New York: Oxford University Press, 1992) p. 85.

34. Ibid.

35. Ibid, pp. 68-9.

36. Ibid., pp. 68-9.

37. The World Bank, *World Development Report 1991*, (New York: Oxford University Press, 1991).

38. Masood Ahmed and Lawrence H. Summers, "The Lessons of the Debt Crisis," *International Economic Insights*, July/August 1992, p. 19.

39. The Development Assistance Committee (DAC) is a select subgroup of the OECD composed of countries that have agreed to secure an expansion of aggregate resources to developing countries and to improve the effectiveness of these resources. The DAC consists of eighteen OECD nations and the Commission of the European Communities. *United Nations Development Report 1992*. p. 6.

40. Summers, p. 7.

41. World Bank, World Debt Tables.

42. Organization for Economic Cooperation and Development, OECD Development Reports 1988, 1991.

43. *Human Development Report*, 1992, pp. 44-5.

44. These distinctions into income categories are based on the following 1991 World Bank classifications; Low income countries are those with a GNP per capita less than $580 in 1989, lower middle income countries' GNP per capita is between $580 and $2335, upper middle countries' are between $2335 and $6000, and upper income countries are above $6000.

45. This is primarily a function of the large disbursements of aid to Israel and Egypt.

46. Robert L. Curry, Jr., "A Review of Contemporary U.S. Foreign Aid Policies," *Journal of Economic Literature*, September, 1990, pp. 815-816.

47. J.F.O. McAllister, "Who Pays the Price" *Time* May 11, 1992.

48. A CED subcommittee is currently undertaking a project on Energy and the Environment that will address many of these issues.

49. *World Development Report 1992*

50. Ibid.

51. Bruce Rich, "Conservation Woes at the World Bank," *The Nation*, 1/23/89.

52. *United Nations Development Report, 1992*, pp. 63-4.

CHAPTER FOUR

1. Which may include such variable contributions as energy, the services of plant and equipment, and materials.

2. John H. Bishop, "Is Test Score Decline Responsible for the Productivity Growth Decline?", *American Economic Review*, March 1989.

3. While women with only 12 years of education saw their incomes rise modestly in this period, this number is probably influenced by the breakdown of legal and cultural barriers in this same period.

4. Ruggles and Stone, p. 25.

5. *An America That Works*, p. 5.

6. See remarks by Frank P. Doyle at the Committee for Economic Development 50th Anniversary Symposium, May 29, 1992.

7. Committee for Economic Development, *An Assessment of American Education*, (New York: CED, 1992)

8. For a more detailed analysis of education reform, see the CED policy statements: *Investing in Our Children, Business and the Public Schools* (1985); *Children in Need: Investment Strategies for the Educationally Disadvantaged* (1987); and *The Unfinished Agenda: A New Vision for Child Development and Education* (1991). For a discussion of the role of business in education reform, see also *Business Impact on Education and Child Development Reform* (1991).

9. This reduction in poverty among the elderly was largely accomplished through the liberalization of Social Security in the 1970s.

10. U.S. Department of Commerce, Bureau of the Census, *Statistical Abstract of the United States*, 1975, 1979, 1985.

11. Lucille Newman, *Preventable Causes of Learning Disabilities*, (Denver: Education Commission of the States, 1991).

12. *An America That Works*, pp. 19-20.

13. U.S. Department of Commerce, Bureau of the Census, *Poverty in the United States* (Washington: Government Printing Office, 1991).

14. National Center on Education and the Economy, *America's Choice, Low Skills or High Wages*, (Rochester, N.Y.: National Center on Education and the Economy, 1990).

15. Ibid.

16. Robert L. Crain, Amy L. Heebner and Yiu-Pong Si, *The Effectiveness of New York City's Career Magnet Schools: An Evaluation of Ninth Grade Performance Using an Experimental Model* (Berkeley: National Center for Research in Vocational Education, 1992).

17. *An America That Works*, p.98

18. Competitiveness Policy Council, p. 14.

19. William J. Baumol, Sue Anne Batey Blackman, and Edward N. Wolf, *Productivity and American Leadership: The Long View*, (Cambridge, MA: The MIT Press, 1989), pp. 262-3.

20. Ibid., p. 15.

21. Robert Buderi, "Global Innovation: Who's in the Lead?," *Business Week*, August 3, 1992, p. 68.

22. *The New York Times*, March 22, 1991, p. D2.

23. National Academy of Engineering, *National Interests in an Age of Global Technology*, (Washington: National Academy Press, 1991) p. 5.

24. Mary Ellen Mogee, *Technology Policy and Critical Technologies*, Discussion Paper 3, prepared for the Manufactuing Forum (Washington: National Academy Press, 1992)

25. Lewis M. Branscomb, "Toward a U.S. Technology Policy," *Issues in Science and Technology*, Summer 1991, pp. 50.

26. MIT Commission on Industrial Productivity, *Made in America*, (New York, Harper Perennial, 1990) p.87.

27. Alfred Malabre, "Economic Roadblock: Infrastructure Neglect," *Wall Street Journal*, July 30, 1990.

28. The MIT Commission on Industrial Productivity, *Made in America*, (New York, Harper Perennial, 1990) p. 111

29. Council on Competitiveness, *Capital Choices: Changing the Way America Invests in Industry*, a research report presented to the Council on Competitiveness and co-sponsored by the Harvard Business School, (Washington: Council on Competitiveness, 1992) p. 26

30. The MIT Commission on Industrial Productivity.

31. Council on Competitiveness, p. 26

MEMORANDA OF COMMENT, RESERVATION, OR DISSENT

Page 10, RODERICK M. HILLS

I do not wish to be associated with the implied criticism of the United States' role in the Gulf War or with the vague call in the same paragraph for a new kind of "collective security structure capable of responding to future threats." A substantial part of the world and most of the world's leaders have applauded the role of America in "rallying" the United Nations behind the ouster of Iraq from Kuwait. Instead of citing this act of demonstrated leadership as an example of the role we expect the United States to play in the future, we damn it with faint praise, saying that it "might not be the precise model" for the future.

Nor is it worthy of us to suggest that there is some structure that could be created that would be more capable of dealing with future Iraqs. What is it? Are we implying that some world body can have a military force capable of dealing with Iraqi-type aggression, or that we would let a force of the size we used in Iraq to be led by an authority not subject to our President? I do not believe that such a body could be created or that we would provide the bulk of a military force without commending it ourselves.

Page 31, RODERICK M. HILLS, with which HARRY L. FREEMAN and FRANKLIN A. LINDSAY have asked to be associated.

By minimizing NAFTA we support the protectionists who want no new trade agreements. More important the economic benefits the United States has already had from liberalization of the Mexican economy over the past three years are clearly quite substantial. Our current $12 billion trade surplus with Mexico is ample evidence that the economic benefits must be substantial if only for the reason that the NAFTA treaty will institutionalize the inroads we have made to date.

Page 31, WALTER Y. ELISHA

Unfortunately, the statement does not emphasize the importance of the Free Trade Agreement (NAFTA). The reality of this agreement is that it provides both a counterweight to the European, Asian and other regional alliances and, more importantly, offers the prospects of creating trade, jobs, and a hemispheric framework for mutual security that otherwise would not exist. Certainly the Uruguay Round, if it is ever concluded, would not provide the same impetus for growth in this hemisphere that the NAFTA promises.

Perhaps the report's alleged "trade-diverting" result of NAFTA could be beneficial if it creates growth and markets for U.S. firms while providing a means for Mexico and ultimately the rest of Latin America to become experienced, fully competitive partners in the global economy. Too, if NAFTA diverts exports from predatory non-market economies away from our markets, that can be an instructive message to such nations — a message that has not been transmitted at high volume in the Uruguay Round market access discussions to date.

I agree we should champion more open global trade, but we can be the "rallier of nations" only if we do so with the confidence that our economic house, as well as the rest of the neighborhood, is strong.

Page 32, RODERICK M. HILLS

The United States is to be commended for stating that it is open to a free trade agreement with any nation prepared to do the same.

Page 33, WILLIAM D. EBERLE

While I agree with the policy directions stated in (1) and (2) in principle, it is important to note that the different natures of the capitalistic systems between Europe, Japan and the United States will make the long-term aim of integration of the world economy an adjustment, which may require some changes in the operation of our system in addition to adjustments by other major nations. Europe and Japan make up a larger share of the world market and have differences in such areas as the technology and R&D support by government, information collection and projected vision by government interventions in various sectors, taxation, competition policies, and more intervention in the investment and financial markets. The language of "the capitalistic market economy," is the same but these differences produce a different result and allow more highly competitive results in favor of other countries. This suggests that the United States, in order to be competitive and to move toward open trade in the world markets, must consider the various aspects and the results therefrom of the differences in the capitalistic system. As important as all of these matters is converging economic policy. The U.S. problems preventing convergence of open and competitive markets include unsustainable federal budget deficit, export restraints, and taxation, which if not addressed promptly, will prevent convergence and leadership by the United States.

Page 35, FRANKLIN A. LINDSAY

The world will experience still another competing demand for capital to process pollutant wastes, to provide clean air and water, and to slow global warming. Until recently, the world's total pollutant loads could be dumped safely into the oceans, into the air, and onto land because they were still small enough to be absorbed without damaging effect. Water could be obtained from local wells, streams, and rivers. Now, pure water must be brought from as far as a thousand miles to metropolitan areas, distilled from sea water, or recycled from waste water. The seas, the atmosphere, and the land can no longer absorb huge volumes of untreated wastes.

Page 78, ELMER B. STAATS, with which FRANKLIN A. LINDSAY and JOSEPH E. KASPUTYS have asked to be associated.

Reduction in outlays for the Department of Defense is having a major impact on the U.S. Defense Industrial Base. While defense technology will continue to have an impact on commercial technology, the defense technology base will be increasingly dependent on developments in the larger and more dynamic commercial sector. With this in mind, more government support for dual-use technology will benefit both the defense and the industrial sectors of the economy.

OBJECTIVES OF THE COMMITTEE FOR ECONOMIC DEVELOPMENT

For over forty years, the Committee for Economic Development has been a respected influence on the formation of business and public policy. CED is devoted to these two objectives:

To develop, through objective research and informed discussion, findings and recommendations for private and public policy that will contribute to preserving and strengthening our free society, achieving steady economic growth at high employment and reasonably stable prices, increasing productivity and living standards, providing greater and more equal opportunity for every citizen, and improving the quality of life for all.

To bring about increasing understanding by present and future leaders in business, government, and education, and among concerned citizens, of the importance of these objectives and the ways in which they can be achieved.

CED's work is supported by private voluntary contributions from business and industry, foundations, and individuals. It is independent, non-profit, nonpartisan, and nonpolitical.

Through this business-academic partnership, CED endeavors to develop policy statements and other research materials that commend themselves as guides to public and business policy; that can be used as texts in college economics and political science courses and in management training courses; that will be considered and discussed by newspaper and magazine editors, columnists, and commentators; and that are distributed abroad to promote better understanding of the American economic system.

CED believes that by enabling business leaders to demonstrate constructively their concern for the general welfare, it is helping business to earn and maintain the national and community respect essential to the successful functioning of the free enterprise capitalist system.

CED BOARD OF TRUSTEES

CED HONORARY TRUSTEES

STATEMENTS ON NATIONAL POLICY ISSUED BY THE COMMITTEE FOR ECONOMIC DEVELOPMENT

SELECTED PUBLICATIONS:

The Economy and National Defense: Adjusting to Cutbacks in the Post-Cold War Era *(1991)*

Politics, Tax Cuts and the Peace Dividend *(1991)*

The Unfinished Agenda: A New Vision for Child Development and Education *(1991)*

Foreign Investment in the United States: What Does It Signal? *(1990)*

An America That Works: The Life-Cycle Approach to a Competitive Work Force *(1990)*

Breaking New Ground in U.S. Trade Policy *(1990)*

Battling America's Budget Deficits *(1989)*

*Strengthening U.S.-Japan Economic Relations *(1989)*

Who Should Be Liable? A Guide to Policy for Dealing with Risk *(1989)*

Investing in America's Future: Challenges and Opportunities for Public Sector Economic Policies *(1988)*

Children in Need: Investment Strategies for the Educationally Disadvantaged *(1987)*

Finance and Third World Economic Growth *(1987)*

Toll of the Twin Deficits *(1987)*

Reforming Health Care: A Market Prescription *(1987)*

Work and Change: Labor Market Adjustment Policies in a Competitive World *(1987)*

Leadership for Dynamic State Economies *(1986)*

Investing in our Children: Business and the Public Schools *(1985)*

Fighting Federal Deficits: The Time for Hard Choices *(1985)*

Strategy for U.S. Industrial Competitiveness *(1984)*

Strengthening the Federal Budget Process: A Requirement for Effective Fiscal Control *(1983)*

Productivity Policy: Key to the Nation's Economic Future *(1983)*

Energy Prices and Public Policy *(1982)*

Public-Private Partnership: An Opportunity for Urban Communities *(1982)*

Reforming Retirement Policies *(1981)*

Transnational Corporations and Developing Countries: New Policies for a Changing World Economy *(1981)*

Fighting Inflation and Rebuilding a Sound Economy *(1980)*

Stimulating Technological Progress *(1980)*

Helping Insure Our Energy Future: A Program for Developing Synthetic Fuel Redefining
   Government's Role in the Market System (1979)

Improving Management of the Public Work Force: The Challenge to State and Local Government (1978)

Jobs for the Hard-to-Employ: New Directions for a Public-Private Partnership *(1978)*

An Approach to Federal Urban Policy *(1977)*

Key Elements of a National Energy Strategy *(1977)*

Nuclear Energy and National Security *(1976)*

Fighting Inflation and Promoting Growth *(1976)*

Improving Productivity in State and Local Government *(1976)*

*International Economic Consequences of High-Priced Energy *(1975)*

Broadcasting and Cable Television: Policies for Diversity and Change *(1975)*

Achieving Energy Independence *(1974)*

A New U.S. Farm Policy for Changing World Food Needs *(1974)*

Congressional Decision Making for National Security *(1974)*

*Toward a New International Economic System: A Joint Japanese-American View *(1974)*

*Statements issued in association with CED counterpart organizations in foreign countries.

CED COUNTERPART ORGANIZATIONS

Close relations exist between the Committee for Economic Development and independent, nonpolitical research organizations in other countries. Such counterpart groups are composed of business executives and scholars and have objectives similar to those of CED, which they pursue by similarly objective methods. CED cooperates with these organizations on research and study projects of common interest to the various countries concerned. This program has resulted in a number of joint policy statements involving such international matters as energy, East-West trade, assistance to developing countries, and the reduction of nontariff barriers to trade.

CE	Circulo de Empresarios Madrid, Spain
CEDA	Committee for Economic Development of Australia Sydney, Australia
CEPES	Vereinigung für Wirtschaftlichen Fortschritt E.V. Frankfurt, Germany
FORUM	Forum de Administradores de Empresas Lisbon, Portugal
IE	Institut de L'Entreprise Brussels, Belgium
IE	Institut de l'Entreprise Paris, France
IEA	Institute of Economic Affairs London, England
IW	Institut der Deutschen Wirtschaft Cologne, Germany
経済同友会	Keizai Doyukai Tokyo, Japan
SNS	Studieförbundet Naringsliv och Samhälle Stockholm, Sweden